DIVINELY

ELEGANT

DIVINELY ELEGANT

THE WORLD OF ERNST DRYDEN

Anthony Lipmann

Foreword by
Billy Wilder

PAVILION
MICHAEL JOSEPH

First published in Great Britain in 1989 by
PAVILION BOOKS LIMITED
196 Shaftesbury Avenue, London WC2H 8JL
in association with Michael Joseph Limited
27 Wrights Lane, Kensington, London W8 5TZ

Designed by Lawrence Edwards

Library of Congress Catalog Card Number: 88-83973

British Library Cataloguing in Publication Data
Lipmann, Anthony
Divinely elegant; the world of Ernst Dryden
I. Austrian graphic arts. Dryden Ernst, 1887-1938. Biographies
I. Title
760'.092'4

ISBN 1 85145 236 2

Photoset by Dorchester Typesetting Group Ltd.
Colour orgination by C.L.G., Verona, Italy.
Printed in Italy by Amilcare Pizzi S.p.A.

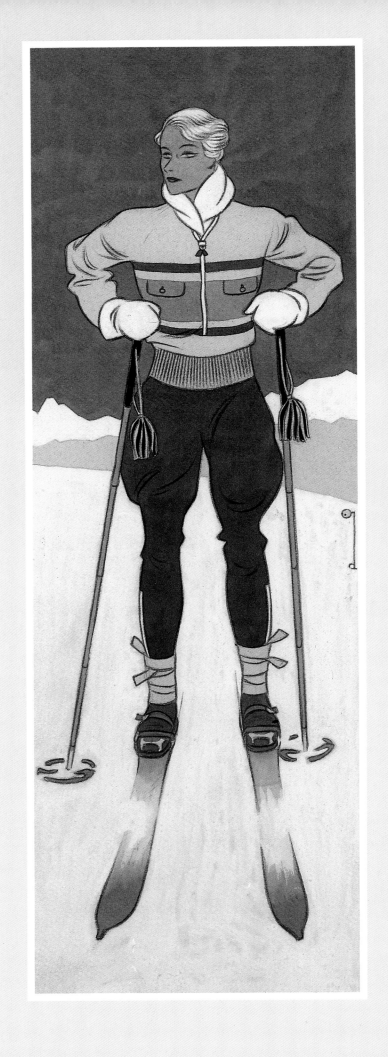

CONTENTS

W H E N W E speak of Ernst Dryden – and we often do, although he has been gone for exactly fifty years – the word that keeps popping up again and again is the word *elegance*. What is elegance? Let me put it this way: either you are born with it or you better forget it. You can't buy it – not at Harrod's or Van Cleef and Arpel's – and you can't fake it, because you'll only be making an ass of yourself. When God spread it around, he sure had his stingy day: a drop of charm here, a touch of style there, but that's all. One in ten thousand got lucky, the rest of us – zilch.

Ernst Dryden had it all, in spades. Consider for instance the way he died. It was sometime in March of '38, we were having a preview at the old Paramount Theatre all the way downtown. The picture was *Bluebeard's Eighth Wife*; Lubitsch was the director, and I was one of the writers. Previews are always unnerving experiences, especially if it's a comedy. It doesn't hurt to have a handful of chums around to enliven the ambience, to augment the laughs, or to shriek occasionally to wake those who have dared doze off.

Dryden was among the ones I had invited, but he did not show up. Very odd. Not like Dryden at all. Maybe he had lost his way, maybe he was in an accident. I found a telephone in the lobby and called him. His line was busy. I called him again, busy again. I called every five minutes. Busy, busy. The movie had started by now. I sat down in the last row, trying to concentrate on the screen, but my mind was on Dryden. An alarm signal had gone off in the pit of my stomach. I began to sweat. In the next seat to me was Bronislav Kaper (we called him Bronek), a very talented composer working at Metro. I tapped his shoulder and whispered my apprehensions. He and his wife, Lola, immediately got up and left. Later he told me what had happened.

They had run to the parking lot and driven off as fast as they could, ignoring the red lights. Dryden's new house was in Westwood, forty-five minutes from the theatre. They made it in twenty and when they arrived the place was shrouded in darkness. No sound from within except the buzzing of the phone. They rang the doorbell, knocked on windows, finally jumped the back fence, and broke through the rear window using one of his pool chairs.

As they made their way through the house toward the buzzing phone everything seemed in perfect order, just the way fastidious Dryden liked it.

At first they did not see him, but then, as they turned toward his favourite black-and-white-checked wing chair, there he was, the receiver by his hand. He was wearing nothing but his white terrycloth robe, dark blue knee socks and one shoe. Whatever happened to him must have occurred before he could put on the other shoe. There was no pulse; he was dead all right.

Meanwhile, I had sat uncomfortably through the preview and at the end I didn't wait around but immediately joined Bronek and Lola at the house. There I found what had happened . . .

That last call – who was he trying to reach? Not a doctor, because for all we knew, he neither had nor needed one. Surely not an ambulance – he would have hated the clamour of sirens, the screeching brakes, the curious neighbours, all of that racket. He would have much preferred the quiet, unobtrusive exit of a very private man.

When we laid him to rest, we finally found out what was wrong: he had been suffering from Graves' Disease (known in Europe as Basedow's), an affliction of the thyroid gland which leads to the production of excess hormones, sometimes manifested by an emotional trauma, and often causing a stroke or heart attack.

In Hollywood, Dryden stayed at the Garden of Allah (he was the only one of the refugees who could afford it), the 'in' place of the 1930s and '40s, an impressive circle of adobe bungalows (style: early Wallace Beery) surrounding a huge pool big enough to drown a herd of rhinoceroses. I was living at the Chateau Marmont right across the street, in a modest room with a Murphy bed and no pool. Dryden, whom I had met casually in Berlin, invited me to use the pool whenever I wanted.

We would be lying there in the sun, soaking up the rays. I always thought him to be extremely good-looking, in a special kind of way. He was on the small side, five feet seven or so, but always trim, always sunburned, reminding me of some exotic, royal prince, Assyrian maybe, with his wild shock of thick, black, curly hair, always tied back with a blue polka-dot bandana to hold it in place.

He brought up that funny day in Berlin when we had lunch at the Café Jaedike on Kochstrasse, right down the street from the Ullstein Verlag. There were three of us: Erich Maria Remarque, the chief editor of *Die Dame* (a sumptuous fashion magazine of the order of *Vogue*), and Dryden, the incomparable illustrator, and finally there was twenty-one-year-old me, a beardless reporter for the noontime paper.

Suddenly, out of the blue, Remarque informed us that he was quitting. Both Dryden and I thought he was crazy. He had by far the best job around: beautiful models, no editorials and a deadline only once a month. Why quit?

Actually, it was Remarque's wife who wanted him to quit. She wanted him to write the novel he had been thinking about. Novel? Who needs another novel? What the hell is it about?

It was about the war. Jesus, Erich, we told him, you're making like 5,000 Marks a month; you're sitting in a tub of butter. Well, we fought like tigers, but ultimately Erich would not listen. The next day, he cleaned out his desk, went home and started writing *All Quiet on the Western Front*. Son of a bitch.

Once Dryden showed me sketches for the costumes he was designing for a David Selznick picture starring Marlene Dietrich. Though it was one of the first colour pictures, he tried desperately to keep it from looking like an ice-cream parlour with twenty-one flavours.

Or sometimes I would try out a plot on him for a new picture. What I thought I needed was a third act – until he convinced me that it was the first and second acts that stunk. Or I would talk about Austria and the inevitable *Anschluss*. When was it coming? His only comment was, the sooner the better, let it be.

I remember at one time he came along with me to my tailor, Eddie Schmidt, the best one in town. He supervized the cut, giving strict instructions on how a double-breasted coat should look. The pockets and lower buttons had to be in *exactly* the same line, down to the last fraction of an inch, and the collar had to be low, so as to show the shirt. The lapels had to have a certain width and a certain shape to give it the proper curve. The material was altogether too thick. On the other hand, the material should not be too thin, or the pants would wrinkle. Then there was an additional twenty-five minutes discussing the lining. What he was lecturing about was exactly the Dryden suit. He must have had two dozen of them, no pinstripes, no plaids. I never got my suit because they could never find the right material. Or more accurately, they didn't want to.

Then there was the short lecture on how to handle a foulard. According to Dryden, you never, absolutely never, look in the mirror. You pick it up in the

Photograph of Dryden at home with friends in the summer of 1937.

1 **Karl Vollmöller (author of *The Miracle*)**
2 **Steffi Duna (actress)**
3 **Hans Szekely (writer)**
4 **Billy Wilder**
5 **Peter Lorre**
6 **Mrs Peter Lorre (Lilly Lwovski)**
7 **Geza Herzeg (writer)**
8 **Ernst Dryden**

centre, shake it out and thrust it into your breast pocket. That's it. You must refrain from fiddling around with it.

Sometime in late '37, he bought himself a neat, small house in Westwood. I helped him with the moving, just me, a couple of friends, and a very pleasant elderly black maid, with whom he seemed to have a great rapport. Meticulous as he was, it took him a whole week placing the lovely Austrian and Bavarian antiques he had had sent over from Europe. Come to think of it, he never talked about women, but after he died, a handsome lady in her middle forties appeared from Europe to dispose of the estate.

I was lucky enough to buy a few of his pieces, not that I needed them to remind me of Dryden – whoever could forget him?

B I L L Y   W I L D E R

*I*T WAS THE long hot summer of 1976 when my great-aunt died. She was 76 years old and had lived in Walton-on-Thames since just before the Second World War.

Little did I or my family realize that below the eaves of her house lay a large part of the life's work of Austrian artist Ernst Dryden, her lifelong friend, who had died in Hollywood in 1938. Thus when I went over to the house on that morning in June I was more than surprised to see part of the contents of the attic strewn across the rubble heap outside the house. It appeared the gardener had been asked to clear out the house and had followed his instructions meticulously.

What I saw before me were sheaves of paper, piled one on top of each other, some turned over or spilling out from one of the two travelling trunks which had been their makeshift time-capsule for the previous 38 years. In spite of having spent the previous twelve hours in the open air, everything was surprisingly undamaged. The greatest luck of all was that it hadn't rained. With the help of a friend I heaved the contents back into the large 1930s-style travelling cases and took them back inside.

As we leafed through the pages and peered inside the folders, some with the artist's arabic looking handwriting scrawled across the covers, what we saw seemed as fascinating as if we had opened a chest containing pieces of eight. There before us we saw dress designs with fabric samples of chiffons or gold or silver lamés, original advertisement designs for Bugatti and Cinzano. Letters spelling the name Dietrich were pencilled on the edge of a film costume design, and pictures of elegant women adorned what I later knew to be front covers of the German magazine *Die Dame*. Nothing was framed. Everything appeared to be exactly as it had been placed in the trunks thirty-eight years previously.

In the following years, I was able to piece together the story. The artist was Ernst Dryden (1887-1938), and he had been one of the finest commercial artists of his generation. Only the turmoils of Europe and his death in America in the months immediately prior to the Second World War had meant that his work had been almost forgotten. But something had ultimately saved it. It had been sent in the two travelling trunks, not back to his native Vienna but to England, where Helene Wolff, his lifelong friend and my great aunt, had stored it away.

What was inadvertently preserved was not only the career of Ernst Dryden but also a picture of life in the 1920s and 1930s seen through the work of a commercial artist whose task it had been to express the elegance of a whole era through his multifarious talents.

The most striking aspect of the work was its variety and volume. It consisted of over four thousand items, including photographs, tracings, sketches, finished gouache artworks, watercolour and pencil designs and many more ephemera. It was in effect the artist's personal collection of his work – a studio of fashion.

From his original work I was able to trace his career through the many twists and turns which had finally led him to America and Hollywood – something which, without the discovery of the collection, would have been impossible.

As the research progressed, I soon discovered that Ernst Dryden had been, under his original name, Ernst Deutsch, one of the foremost poster artists in Germany. With this information, I was able to look in German and Continental museums where I found over 192 items housed there as well as two items in the Victoria & Albert Museum in London. I was able to make an outline of his career and it ran as follows:

Born Ernst Deutsch on 3 August 1887 in Vienna of Hungarian parents, he

A GALLERY FOUND IN A GARDEN

became famous as a poster artist in Berlin between 1910 and 1918. He served in the First World War as an officer in the Imperial Flying Corps, winning the Iron Cross. Upon returning to Berlin after the war, and finding that town in the throes of defeat and revolution, he left, moving back to Vienna and changing his name to Dryden. Here he began a new career as menswear designer to the firm of tailors and outfitters Knize, for whom he supplied designs from his studio on Trattnerhof. In 1926 he accepted a commission to work for *Die Dame*, the German equivalent of *Vogue*, moving his base to Paris, the centre of *haute couture*. This lasted until 1933 when he left for New York, working there for a year as a dress designer, before finally gravitating to Hollywood in 1934, where he started work as a costumier for several major films. He died in Hollywood in 1938.

In the course of his career Dryden worked in most of the key commercial media of his day but, as if strapped to the wheel of fashion, he was continually impelled to move on, working in the most competitive media at any one particular time. It had made his career hard, if not impossible, to follow. Had it not been for the gallery in the garden it would not have been possible to tell the story of Dryden's eventful life and to reveal the lost world of elegance which he reflected.

Illustration from *Die Dame* showing the new season's fabrics in the form of a collage circa 1927.

STREIFEN

KAROS

TUPFEN

FEN

TUPFEN

TUPF

THE DRYDEN PERSONA

'Er war geleckt!' — he looked as if he had been licked all over by a cat.

HE WAS NOT tall, but he wanted to be. His hair was slightly curly so each night he wore a bandana to keep it pressed to his scalp. Elegant? In an age that appreciated elegance 'he was the most elegant man who ever lived!'

He was a proud, witty man, who was always good company. To those younger than him he was a teacher — there was a need in him almost to preach the techniques of his art as if by this act he redoubled his own efforts. He believed in work, hard work. Finally, he believed in one thing above all — 'himself'.

It would normally be regarded as unusual to find among people's private documents a considerable number of photographs of themselves. But among the Dryden papers were several photograph albums, with black and white pictures carefully stuck down, all pictures of 'himself' — Dryden.

A photograph from about 1921 in Vienna shows him standing in front of large white wooden double-doors. He is besuited, white-cuffed hands in pockets, the flourish of a white handkerchief in his breast-pocket. His expression is utterly 'posed' or 'composed'. Eyelids heavy and eyebrows slightly raised, arrogantly elegant. It is the sort of photographic still a film star might have. But this photograph is not unique. It is one of over a hundred photographs of himself.

Vanity? Yes, perhaps, but something more too. Dryden, dress and menswear designer, was his own first test of elegance. That he was not as tall or perfect a model as he would have liked to be was a frustration. But this did not prevent him from exercising his own iron rules of fashion as rigidly on himself as on anyone else. The designer of men's clothes could not look anything other than perfectly dressed. He was his own object of elegance which he believed in and which was his cardinal starting point — the Dryden persona, the elegant man.

This obsession for self-promotion may be seen in all that he did. His personality was his own trademark. He was an advertisement for himself. And, in fact, it literally produced business for him. Even in the letters he wrote he often used the third person singular. Not 'I . . .', but 'Dryden . . .', 'he'.

In 1913, at the age of 26, he was invited to make a pictorial entry in the visitors' book of the Berlin poster collector, Dr Hans Sachs. All the members of Dr Sachs's circle, some of the greatest poster artists of the day, including Julius Klinger, Ludwig Hohlwein, Lucien Bernhard and Julius Gipkens, all made their entries in the book. Dryden's entry is a self-portrait — a picture of his almost dandyish 'self'. The sketch in ink against a green background is of a supremely posed figure with stick, hat and tails 'as if arriving at the party'. Again the face is posed and deliberately unsmiling, but not serious. The eyes are emphasized, suggesting blackened rims caused by Shelley-esque overwork and fragile youth. It is a masterpiece of self-expression and confidence, and shows that even in 1913 Dryden already saw himself in this somewhat dramatic context. Even at the time of this entry, the entire March 1913 issue of an advertising publication called *Mitteilungen des Vereins Deutscher Reklamefachleute* (News from the Association of German Advertising Experts) was devoted to him as the rising star of poster art in Austria and Germany.

Soon his posters (signed Deutsch) were to appear all over Germany, and the other expression of himself — his actual signature with the first and last letters written as if in dripping blood — was a common sight on all the hoardings.

If there is a theme that runs throughout his career, it is this: the belief in himself that never failed him, the belief that all his powers lay within him. Nor was this confidence misplaced: his powers as an artist were a flame which he could take

Previous page
Front and back cover of an advertising trade journal, Berlin, March 1913.

with him from country to country and which finally took him near the end of his life to America.

Ernst Dryden was born ten years before Gustav Klimt led his group away from the Vienna Academy and formed the Secession. Both his parents were Hungarian, his father coming from the town of Szegedin and mother from Budapest. The family name was 'Deutsch' and this was the name under which Dryden originally became well known, as a poster artist in Austria and Germany. He had a sister and brother. Lili Maté, nine years his senior and Fritz, six years younger. Although of Hungarian descent he did not speak with an accent. Indeed his German was closer to the language spoken in Germany and unlike the preciousness of Vienna.

EARLY
Y E A R S

According to Ottokar Mascha in his book *Österreichische Plakatkunst* (Austrian Poster Art), published in 1915, Dryden was educated at the Kunstgewerbeschule (The Vienna School of Arts and Crafts) and was a pupil of Gustav Klimt. As Mascha was the first to organize a poster exhibition in the Secession building in 1912, and Klimt was still alive at the time of this book, there is no reason to doubt his claim. Certainly, many years later Dryden was a regular visitor to the school at prize-giving day and as a later student, Eric Stapler, has recalled, Dryden was the most admired of all those that came to speak and the one that they most wished to emulate.

Effectively, Dryden's career grew out of the ferment of Vienna in the last days of the Austro-Hungarian Empire, when writers, artists, musicians, and architects, as well as the new psychoanalysts, contributed to the life of that city in a way that has not been seen before or since.

Dryden's career follows an idiosyncratic path through the movements of the day, but in broad terms his work comes under the heading of commercial art. While the outspoken artists and philosophers of the day were writing tracts and calling for art to move out of the stultifying atmosphere of the Academy – the Secessionists and later Bauhaus craved the growing together of Arts and Crafts and praised the likes of England's William Morris and John Ruskin – it was in effect artists like Dryden who put some of these ideas into practice. In his career he was to move with the fashions, work and excel in at least five media and at no stage indulge in the fantasies of some of his mainstream peers. He was the true applied artist.

Although born and educated in Vienna, like a number of other Austrians of talent, the real flowering of Dryden's early career (as Ernst Deutsch) in fact began in Berlin. Other Austrians to make the trip included the famous theatre director Max Reinhardt, and poster artists Julius Klinger and Lucien Bernhard, with whom Dryden worked closely amongst the circle of artists who received commissions via the printing works of Hollerbaum & Schmidt.

THE
G O L D E N
A G E
O F
P O S T E R S

In 1910, at the time Dryden made his move, Berlin had a lot more to offer. Larger than Vienna, it was also less parochial, and its population had more spending power for the new products which poster artists were commissioned to advertise.

In the development of poster art, Germany had previously been behind France, whose Jules Cheret still was its most illustrious pioneer, but from about 1909 onwards the environment in Germany was ripe for its further development.

The differences between France and Germany are worth noting. France's poster art had developed faster because of the greater freedom in society. This showed itself particularly in the freedom to portray women. Jules Cheret's women figures, who effectively became his signature tune, were called 'Cherettes' and they were eagerly awaited and loved by their street audiences. On top of this the wide range of theatre and dance entertainments of *belle époque* Paris caused a need for advertising that the poster fulfilled. Furthermore, the involvement in poster art of great artists like Henri de Toulouse Lautrec or Theophile Alexandre Steinlen, whether attracted by the money or the subject matter, could not but raise the humble poster on to a higher plane.

However, when the energy of the poster began to sweep Germany in 1909, it came about for different reasons. In Germany it would never quite be possible to be as free as Cheret when it came to entertainment subjects; but Germany was the first country truly to harness the power of poster art to industry.

In this regard, Dryden was not the follower of a long German tradition in poster art but one of a then small circle of powerful original artists who were pioneers. Dryden soon established his niche within this world as he became known from this time onwards as the master of fashion. What the German poster artists did was to work in very close contact with industry, answering to industry's real demands and managing to produce posters which served their advertising purpose and did not have to show off the artist's credentials as a painter.

It was a turning-point in poster art, the moment where fine art and posters split. It would not be possible any longer for the fine artist to dabble in posters. The poster artist was now a breed of his own, with developing rules that applied only to his art.

In the same year as poster art came of age in Berlin in 1909, it also found a way to discuss the path forward, for this was also the year of the founding of one of the greatest aids to the promotion of poster art in Germany – Dr Hans Sachs's magazine of 'The Poster', *Das Plakat*.

Looking at issues of *Das Plakat* today, it is not difficult to appreciate its influence. Printed on the most lavish papers, each issue was in itself a work of art with articles and images that publicized and discussed every aspect of poster design. In 1915 a year's subscription for six issues payable in advance was fifteen Marks, and for that the subscriber also became a member of the 'Society of the Friends of the Poster'.

The magazine was both academic and philosophical. Its views, summed up by its founder, were contained in the motto 'No more un-artistic posters, no more trashy ads in Germany!' In this somewhat crusading light, *Das Plakat* was created as a forum for discussion on all aspects of poster art for trade and collector alike. There were articles on how posters should be kept, how to collect, and the creation of contacts, for the purpose of swaps; study of poster trends in other countries, including expressions of admiration, particularly of the 'Beggarstaff Brothers', whose works in England were held up as models of poster art; debate as to whether high-class products should have high-class posters, and low-class products, low-class posters.

These discussions were all the product of a new and growing poster art industry into which the name of Deutsch was launched, and where it soon became synonymous with style and elegance.

Dr Sachs and his circle created a forum for the exchange of ideas and self-promotion. It must have been largely successful, as the artists whose works he collected are the most famous poster artists of this period. Sachs seems to have had all the qualities necessary to be a good patron. He was not an artist himself but a precise man, a dentist by profession, whose personal obsession was to champion the poster in all its forms and from whatever source. In this calling he brought to bear a considerable breadth of talent on his publication.

With that same precision he was able to record with some pride in 1915 that he had collected a total of 3,250 posters, out of which 1,962 were German. In his German list, which perhaps shows which posters he regarded then as having most value, either aesthetically or for reasons of posterity, the following artists are prominent: Hohlwein: 145 items; Bernhard: 131; Klinger: 129; Scheurich: 65; Erdt: 64; Deutsch: 58; Gipkens: 47.

This shows that Dryden, relatively young as he was, was amongst his favourite artists. By 1938, when Sachs left Germany for America, his total collection had grown to some 12,500 items and was one of the largest private collections of classic posters ever known to have existed. Sadly, it was lost during the War. All that remains of his collection is his visitors' book, today housed in the Kunstbibliothek Berlin and in which the young Dryden recorded his entry in 1913.

In an issue of the *Mitteilungen des Vereins Deutscher Reklamefachleute* of March 1913, Dryden was accorded for the first time an entire supplement devoted to his work, with introduction by his fellow artist and compatriot Julius Klinger. By writing about each other, they promoted not only themselves but poster art too. Here Klinger highlights for the first time Dryden's lifelong interest in fashion, even though at this stage its main outlet was through posters and not dress design. Klinger notes that Dryden was able to say, 'At last the elegant of Berlin look like my drawings.'

Another contributor to the same issue, E. E. Hermann Schmidt, writing from a businessman's point of view, says something similar, 'I don't know any artist who is as well informed about fashion, who loves fashion as much and is enthusiastic about all the delightful superficies that make up the elegant woman.' What he was highlighting was that in a sense elegance was the great weapon in Dryden's armoury; for if the most mundane products could in some way, by being part of a Deutsch poster, appear elegant they would also therefore be desirable.

The Salamander poster is a good example of this. Here a shoe company, still in existence today, is introducing new high heels. Including within the image the contrasting colours of green for chequerboard type floor and red for the dresses, which are still the firm's colours today, the poster looks at three pairs of elegant ladies' ankles at eye level. The three ladies, whom we can only imagine from their ankles, are about to move in step and as they do we see three beautifully poised heels move off from the floor as if held in a freeze frame. It was a highly successful poster, which was reworked for Salamander's newspaper advertisements, and which may have owed some of its success to the daring eye-level angle with which the viewer sees the new heel – ladies' ankles not being entirely visible at this time.

Linked to this perceived quality of elegance with which advertisers believed Dryden could gild their products was, according to Schmidt, Dryden's grasp of the commercial needs of the advertiser. Klinger had already drawn attention to the way in which artists all too often appeared to produce masterly paintings in isolation and then attempted to marry image to product in an artificial manner. Dryden was wholly unlike this and the business people loved him for it.

Another of his famous posters of this time, his 1911 poster for Mercedes typewriters, shows this clarity of purpose. It is an interesting poster from a number of points of view. Once again, the object to be advertised is mundane enough, but we appear also to see now the top half of one of the ladies who were about to appear in the Salamander poster. (The heels and skirt are exactly the same.) Dryden's composite woman of elegance is seated by the typewriter with head slightly turned. What people in Berlin would also have known is that Dryden's lady seated at the typewriter was based on a similar poster advertising pianos of a few years earlier. In a simple stroke, Dryden has made an important social statement – the woman has been taken away from the stay-at-home environ-ment of the piano and is now a woman of independence earning her living. Lest it be supposed for a moment that this secretary is as much a slave to her social condition as the lady at the piano once was, we must remember that in 1911 most secretaries were male.

Dryden had learnt a lesson about advertising that is as valid today as it was then – that in order to be truly powerful advertising has to appeal to deep social forces. To be successful in the marketplace the products of light industry, whether they be heels or lightbulbs, must not just be modern in design but modern in their application and relationship to people. The typewriter in his poster has become the means of social liberation for the woman. It implies that the woman who sits by the brand of typewriter has freed herself.

Klinger's report on Dryden at this early stage of his career also allows us a sudden glimpse of his character at this time. For he writes, 'When I am asked to speak about Deutsch personally, I am not able to be objective, I like his kind of work too much. He is clever and witty but occasionally displays astonishing unkindness, which sets him pleasantly apart from the all too sweet Viennese.' What this unkindness was, we do not know. Possibly the two men were in competition for the same customers, for posters by both artists exist for Excelsior rubber heels, the Admirals-Palast dance hall, *Die Woche* newspaper and Kupferberg Riesling Champagne.

Klinger rounded off his article as follows: 'His personal elegance is often extreme but will never be taken beyond certain boundaries. . . . It is self-evident that a man like Deutsch who has such great success and who has the courage to go his own way, not with the express desire to make friends, has many opponents, imitators and copiers. The cool and calmness with which he accepts this are proof that he is a splendid person.'

From his *atelier* in Schöneberg, the Dryden creations emerged to be printed mainly at the works of Hollerbaum & Schmidt, the main lithographic printers of Berlin, who produced almost all the best posters of the era. What the exact relationship was between the artist and printer is difficult to say, but certainly in a relatively new art form it was different from today. It seems almost certain that in the first instance it was the printer who obtained the original enquiries and then passed them out to the various artists, whose studios acted like satellites. It was under the banner of Hollerbaum & Schmidt, for example, that Dryden's work would appear at the large trade fairs, alongside the works of their other artists. The owner, Ernst Growald, was the first to be credited with bringing businessmen together with a wider circle of artistic potential, which in turn produced the flowering of Berlin poster life.

Poster artist and advertiser were aided by other circumstances in society too. Berlin in 1912 had a powerful industrial base in both light and heavy industry which needed to advertise its wares, a population hungry for new ideas and with considerable spending power, and over 90 newspapers and periodicals serving

Berlin alone. On a more basic level it also had Litfass poster pillars, named after their inventor, on each street corner on which the entertainments could be easily broadcast. With most people in the metropolis travelling on foot rather than by car, a poster could be seen by thousands of people in a single day.

With film still in its infancy, visual posters became the other great silent art form, and some of the techniques used to communicate a message via silent means were common to each medium. A visual dialogue was created with the people. The poster artist himself was in a position of power, commanding a certain amount of awe, respect and excitement. The same influences which made German films so exciting in the early part of the century were also reflected in poster art. People knew better how to use their eyes to obtain immediate information or pleasure. The way a woman's head was poised, the exact length of a dress would be immediately noticed. In the poster for *Der Leibgardist* (The Guardsman), a play by Franz Molnar, the officer's somewhat small head looks down from a huge body as if to signify the strength of his intelligence.

Another example is the character of the German version of the *femme fatale* figure who later fascinated the world in its screen embodiment as Marlene Dietrich. Not that Dietrich was unique: in the early years of this century women cast in her mould were typical of German nightlife society, but it is difficult to decide which came first. Was the *femme fatale* created by poster artists, were they merely depicting an existing style that mirrored the many facets of Berlin life, or did each influence the other?

Dryden produces the epitome of this female in a number of posters. Most excitingly in the Admirals Casino poster in which three young ladies appear to dance the tango together in a suggestive manner, with interlocking hands outstretched in a pose that has a frisson of sexual daring even when looked at today. She appears again in the Richards Grill series, with shadows around the eyes, red lips and pale skin. She is accompanied in the dance of the tango in the poster called Tabarin, where the man has an element of self-portrait that would suggest it is the artist himself.

We must not forget that when Klinger had said, 'It is Ernst Deutsch who puts his stamp on the elegant of Berlin', he was implying quite an influence. For by saying this one would have to say that Dryden was one of the key creators of that unique Berlin atmosphere which has gone down in contemporary history. Although, in fact this may be saying too much, what he did do is always draw people from life, which also meant that he could be seen late at night sketching at some of the night-spots which later became the subjects of some of his posters.

It was Dryden's faithfulness to life which was reflected in Klinger's remark: 'You can see the meticulously dressed gentlemen and sophisticated ladies at the "Bristol" for breakfast and at the "Grand Gala" for dinner – sadly, real people never attain the charm and quality of his designs!'

By creating a standard of elegance in his posters which depicted men and women not as Mucha classical figures but in real life settings of nightclubs, dance tournaments and restaurants he created an image which the young aspired to. The advertiser was pleased because his product could find a place in a flattering social setting. The public went out and spent their money because they believed that by buying the product they might in a sense become as elegant and wonderful as the poster image.

Not everyone wanted to draw for the fashion trade. Many other German poster artists were just as keen on the machine. A different issue of *Das Plakat*

The shopfront of Kersten & Tuteur, at the heart of Berlin's fashion district on the Leipzigerstrasse with the 'K & T' vignette designed by Dryden visible on the windowpane. Dryden was author of the corporate identity for the store whose lettering and vignette also appear on the posters.

would be devoted to artists whose careers depicted and depended upon communicating the excitement of billowing smokestacks or chemical factories.

A reflection of the extent to which Dryden, in contrast, became pre-eminent in the sphere of fashion is afforded by the visual record his work provides of Berlin's most famous fashion street of this period – the Leipzigerstrasse. In the years before the First World War the street was flourishing after a long period of stability, and just about to respond to the vast changes that were taking place. Dryden executed designs and posters for many of the stores in this street. At No 43, Seidenweberei Michels, the silk house; at No 20-22, F.V. Grünfeld, a linen house; Edmund Wünsch menswear was at 101-102; and finally Kersten & Tuteur – Das Haus der Moden (The House of Fashion) was at No 36.

The last of these, Kersten & Tuteur, only opened on 1 March 1913 and Dryden was intimately involved with its initial planning and promotion. With its imposing building on the corner of Leipzigerstrasse and Charlottenstrasse, it had four floors on which were contained every conceivable requirement in ladies fashion including coats, bed-linen, négligées, underwear, jerseys, aprons, millinery, children's clothes, corsets, blouses, dresses, toiletries and much more. In one of the promotional advertisements, Dryden describes separate departments each with a visual scene, presented within an oval frame.

Dryden's involvement with Kersten & Tuteur also shows another aspect of his work. For he became, in effect, the creator of Kersten & Tuteur's corporate identity. Commissioned for his knowledge as a designer, he would not allow the house style for the store to evolve in a hit-and-miss manner. Instead, with the owner's full backing, Dryden attempted to show that the creation of a strong identity could lead to marketing success. It was something we take for granted now, but which was relatively new then; he co-ordinated the colours of furniture, uniforms for employees and delivery vans, and even the paper bags were designed to carry the firm's vignette. This too – a crest with the letters 'K' and 'T' below a silhouette of a lady in billowing skirts looking into an oval mirror – showed the designer touch.

Kersten & Tuteur wanted to make shopping at their store an exciting and magnificent experience. Once the decor was in place, fashion shows with live models were staged for the first time in Berlin and, as if to avoid any danger of scandal, these shows were turned into small theatrical events called *Theater der Moden* (Theatres of Fashion). A whole play specially written for the firm was performed on 15 March inside their ample premises to parade the styles that would be sold. It was as if, by using the disguise of theatre, the audience would accept that young ladies could dress up and be on show without necessarily being coquettish.

In the same year of 1913 Dryden also executed two further posters for another *Theater der Moden* which was a series of fashion shows between 14 September and 15 October. The wording again advertised the fact of 'mannequins vivants' or 'live models' as never seen before. It seems we must try to imagine the shock of seeing young beautifully dressed ladies moving and breathing rather than the dumb mannequins people were used to. In a little quip on this novelty, Dryden's poster for Erdmannsdorfer Büstenfabrik (1913), a mannequin manufacturer, shows the head tailor hugging a mannequin who appears to be about to come alive.

In the *Theater der Moden* posters, maybe partly to disguise the true purpose of the event, the first image contains the picture of three ladies of which only one is wearing the modern fashion, while in the second picture four figures, including an admiral, look on in mild disdain as the young lady, centre-stage, raises a stockinged leg to reveal a good six inches above the ankle.

Kersten & Tuteur had taken the theatrical experience to its logical conclusion. By creating in their store an Aladdin's cave of fashion, they ensured that entering the building would be a fashion experience. And yet, as if to prove it was not all show, as well as the lavish interior decoration and the roof gardens, the owners made sure that the firm's employees were given excellent conditions in which to work which included shower and refreshment rooms on the top floor.

Dryden's deep involvement with fashion, though, did not consume him entirely. At the same time as all this, he was able to complete posters for over 14 films – posters which form part of the fascinating early history of the film industry. They highlight from another point of view too the vibrancy and idiosyncracy of film-making in Germany at this time – some of whose elements were to emerge in Hollywood years later.

One of its greatest stars at this time was the Danish actress, Asta Nielsen, and Dryden created posters for at least four of her films. One was for the Urban Gad screenplay *Komödianten* (Comedians) in which Dryden depicts her with melancholy, ringed eyes in pierrot costume, hatless and strangely androgynous, with hair covered and obscured by the skull-cap of a clown. Famous for her intense performances of *Hamlet*, Nielsen conformed to the pose of the time that Dryden himself had aspired to in the portrait of himself in Sachs's visitors' book. The pose of burnt-out youth, whose pale tubercular features and unsmiling face are like the mask for deep over-welling feelings.

The script for *Komödianten* appears to have been a vehicle for Nielsen. It is the story of an actress who has an affair with an actor, by whom she has a child. When a new actress takes her part the actor leaves Nielsen for her. Nielsen makes friends with a playwright and is to act in a play called *Pierrot's Death* when her child becomes ill and asks to see his father. On the point of playing the part she hears her child is dying and overcome by the feelings of mother-love returns to her child. When informed by a nurse that her child is dead she returns to the stage for the opening night of *Pierrot's Death* and, in what is meant to be a mock sword fight, she removes the protective cover of the actor's blade and is killed by her former lover unbeknown to the audience.

It was a powerful and bleak story that gripped the thousands of people who went to see it in 1913. When looking at the poster again, we can see that Dryden latched on to the character of Nielsen as the pivotal character around which the whole drama revolves. In embryo, this was the star system of promotion long before Hollywood took the concept to its logical conclusion. In each of the other films, star and part had become one, as the titles suggest: *Die falsche Asta Nielsen* (The False Asta Nielsen), *Das Mädchen ohne Vaterland* (The Girl without a Homeland).

Finally, apart from the medium of posters Dryden was also able to execute at this time a prolific quantity of magazine advertising for some of the many Berlin journals of the day which included *Elegante Welt*, *Seidels Reklame*, *Deutsche Illustrierte Zeitung*, *Jugend* and *Lüstige Blätter*. The smaller format in which these advertisements had to make their impact led him to adapt his art, dispensing with most of the subtleties that are produced by colour. Instead, as if responding to Aubrey Beardsley's dictum, 'How little the importance of outline is understood even by some of the best painters', he produced work in pen and ink which

Asta Nielsen, the Danish actress and star of many early German silent films around the time when Dryden executed a number of film posters featuring her, 1913.

depended entirely upon the simple techniques of drawing.

Beardsley had said this because he knew that his works would be seen for the first time in the printed form of a small book rather than large like a poster or in the privacy of a gallery wall. If this was going to be the case, he knew that the definition of line would come out true when printed, whereas printing techniques would not reproduce subtle tones had he depended upon them. Beardsley simultaneously distanced himself from fine artists who looked down upon commercial art. His use of outline made his distance all the more clear.

When Dryden used this technique it was for the same technical reason. In his journal advertisements it was a highly appropriate style, as may be seen from his striking series for the cigarette firm Manoli, then marketed by Reemtsma, the current owners of the St Moritz brand.

Dryden's time in Berlin should have gone on far longer. Instead, all the work above only corresponds to three or four short years' work between 1910 and 1914. During this time he captured the spirit of Berlin as it was before the First World War, which at that moment, unknown to the world, was the last time Berlin would ever be either truly proud, rich or vibrant.

Very soon the black pall of the First World War would overhang his career and that of thousands of others. It foreshortened Dryden's career in Germany and only intermittent items were produced during the next few years. To add to his troubles, he was one of the principal subjects in a vituperative attack on poster art in Germany which was to have further consequences on the development of his career.

DIE SCHWARZE LISTE

By 1915 Dryden was recruited into the infantry and within a year he had been transferred to the Imperial Flying Corps No 22 Company. For the smart man what other part could he have played? And not even the war could prevent him having some photographs taken of himself to record his progress, posed in flying gear with a dog on his knee complete with goggles, scarf and boots, or in more serious mood looking rather like the Red Baron.

But during this time at the front the up and coming star of German poster art was strongly attacked in a book entitled *Die Schwarze Liste* (The Black List) by Hans Reimann (1916). In an era much given to rough pamphleteering and character assassination, it is an impressive document — 133 pages long, containing 97 illustrations, ten of them being comparisons with works by Deutsch. The author's aim is to reveal what he sees as blatant plagiarism in posters, magazine advertisements and satirical picture design. He sees the copyists as rife and immoral, and with pedantic efficiency he produces examples of similar images on facing pages; 'source' and alleged copied version.

Dryden was not the only artist to stand accused, but he was the most prominent, and Reimann worded his attack on him in no uncertain terms. 'The only genuine thing on a Deutsch poster is his signature,' he said, 'and even this with its distinctive drooping letters is in turn imitated by other artists.' Reimann regarded the whole industry as sick. Dryden was a copier, he believed. But he was a good enough copier to be also the subject of copying.

A painting by Austrian artist, Egger-Lienz, of a child sitting in a chair is compared with a similar child in similar chair by Dryden. A fashion plate from *Gazette du Bon Ton* dated 1913, is contrasted with Dryden's similar item in *Elegante Welt* in 1914. An English advertisement for pianos is put alongside Dryden's famous poster for Mercedes typewriters.

'Although I am a member of "The Society of Friends of the Posters" [The *Das Plakat* Circle],' Reimann declared, 'this is where poster friendship ends . . .'

Like all pamphleteers, Reimann was undoubtedly motivated by a strong animus bordering on envy. He seems also to have felt that in discovering the sources of some of Dryden's designs he had uncovered a plot or conspiracy. With a sense of satisfaction he had found a method of attacking the man at the peak of his popularity – 'The whole of Germany is flooded with his posters – any child with an average intelligence would know him.'

The attack had its desired effect. Dryden, with his back turned while serving at war, was at his most vulnerable. When he finally returned to Berlin he did indeed find his career destroyed. Victor Skutezky, the film producer, who then owned a night-spot in Berlin, recalled that from having earned 100,000 Marks or more a year, he was suddenly shunned and worthless.

Looking back, it is hard to see how a person such as Reimann could have wielded such power. It is even harder to see the truth in what he alleged. However, a whole issue of *Das Plakat*, dated July 1915, was entitled *Das Plakat und Plagiat* (The Poster and Plagiarism).

Rather than looking at Dryden in isolation, whose career was temporarily in pieces, it is possible to see that the wider concerns of plagiarism were a live issue of the day, with accusation and counter-accusation. Although at least one career, Dryden's, was almost permanently destroyed because of it, the subject lingered on and ultimately caused a backlash of rules which stultified the art of the poster and contributed to its gradual decline in importance after the First World War.

What Reimann refused to admit was that forbidding or creating fear in an artist of copying, derivation and parody was rather like telling a composer to create an aria without referring to any part of musical history. If he had really wanted to charge Dryden with plagiarism he should also have cited the advertisement he had devised for Hollerbaum & Schmidt, in which a series of little figures prance about the naked recumbent body of the artistic muse offering their works for praise and judgement. For the design was derived from a classic Roman Sculpture housed in the Vatican, entitled *Il Nilo* and over nine hundred years old! Reimann's attack was based on the foolish proposition that all art should be original; morally tenable but showing scant appreciation of the history of art.

Reimann had chosen to ignore the element of parody with which Dryden would execute a design; nor could he see that the so-called derivative works were numerically only a fraction of Dryden's prolific output.

One of the designs Dryden was accused of plagiarizing was a fashion plate from the French magazine *Gazette du Bon Ton* dated 1913. In fact the original is a fairly unremarkable illustration of a lady wearing a hooped skirt. The picture Reimann compared it with was Dryden's drawing showing the same dress and lady, only this time with the lady holding on to a hoop outside the skirt upon which was hung a row of shoes. Dryden was simply using a familiar but out of date design to make a fashion point. The point quite simply was – 'hoops and corsets are out'. (The hoop was about as much use as a hanger for shoes!)

In spite of the apparently false aim of the person shooting the arrows, it is amusing to note that an invaluable by-product of Reimann's work is his drawing together of Dryden's work and its sources, which from today's vantage point would be almost impossible to trace. It is particularly interesting – rather than damning – to note that Dryden must often have turned to the satirical magazines

Ernst Dryden, a portrait of the fashion designer at war, together with friend, in flying leathers and in battle dress circa 1916.

Simplicissimus and *Assiette au Beurre* for inspiration. Today the comparisons with Dryden's sources provide a fascinating insight into the way he worked, showing in effect how a dull picture could be brought to life or turned to Dryden's humorous purpose.

Perhaps in the early years of advertising this battle was bound to take place. Companies were only just beginning to find that if they employed a designer to make their goods exciting and desirable it could transform their fortunes. The pride of the Victorian era which believed, as it did in England, that a good product was its own best advertisement was about to be superseded. But there were still those, such as Reimann, who represented the moral backlash.

Although Dryden returned from the war having been awarded the Iron Cross for bravery, there were little thanks in Berlin. The year 1918 was an anguished time in that town. The defeated nation was in the throes of revolution and civil strife. There was fighting on the streets, with an attempt to overthrow the elected socialist Government. At the same time his marriage broke up, perhaps as a result of his absence at the war or the destruction of his career. Berlin can have held few pleasures for him then.

With very little money and his career in tatters, he made a break with the past, not only moving to a different country and town – Vienna – but changing his name from Deutsch to Dryden. Why he changed his name and why to *Dryden* is an enigma.

As an artist who was himself the creator of identities, he simply may have wished to create a new identity for himself to mark a new beginning in his career. This he certainly achieved. And yet, if this was the case, why should he have chosen a name that was similar to the American *Vogue* illustrator, Helen Dryden, who was no relation? Why too should he have pronounced the name 'Dreeden', which was neither the German nor English pronunciation of the name?

It seems unlikely that these questions can be answered except by conjecture, but one practical reason for the change of name may have been to avoid litigation from anyone who wished to pursue him with the false plagiarism charges. Perhaps too he wished to distance himself from his broken marriage. Whatever the case, the new Dryden did indeed make a break with the past and it was a life-giving move. He literally left the past behind him and, rather like someone who closes down one firm and opens another, he set about the task of making the firm of Dryden a great success.

From the visitors' book of poster
collector Dr Hans Sachs in watercolour
and ink on paper, 1913.

Following page
Stone lithographic poster from a
Christmas exhibition, Berlin,
December 1913.

WEIHNACHTS-
ALT-B
VOM 4, BIS 28, DEZEMBER 191

Stone lithographic poster for Mercedes
typewriters, 1911.

Previous page
Stone lithographic poster for the
Salamander shoe company, 1912.

Stone lithographic poster for a high school for the art of good cutting, 1911. Note the words 'System le grand chic' advertising French fashion.

Stone lithographic poster for a dance
tournament on January 31st, 1912.

Der Leibgardist

Komödie in 3 Akten
von Franz Molnár

Neues Theater
Frankfurt a./M.
Direktion Hellmer u. Reimann

HOLLERBAUM & SCHMIDT BERLIN N 65

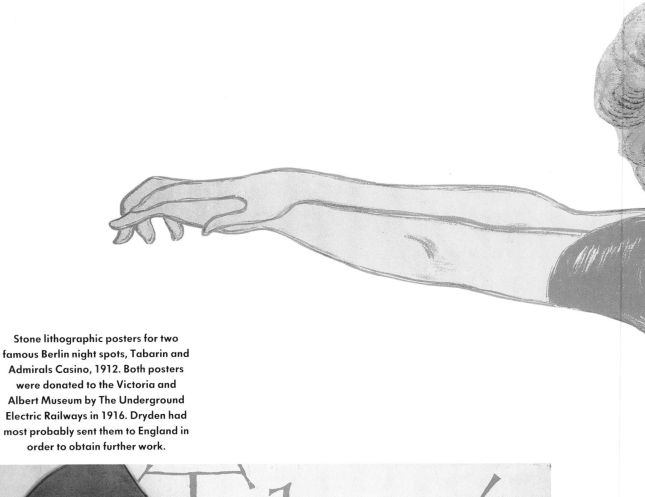

Stone lithographic posters for two famous Berlin night spots, Tabarin and Admirals Casino, 1912. Both posters were donated to the Victoria and Albert Museum by The Underground Electric Railways in 1916. Dryden had most probably sent them to England in order to obtain further work.

Tabarín
Täglich Reunion
Jägerstraße 58.

HOLLERBAUM & SCHMIDT BERLIN N 65

Opposite
Stone lithographic poster for the opening of a new fashion department store, Kersten & Tuteur, Berlin, 1913.

Stone lithographic poster for Richard's Grill, 1913. Twelfth in a series for this meeting place of Berlin Society. Note the design's economy of colour: only black and red are used.

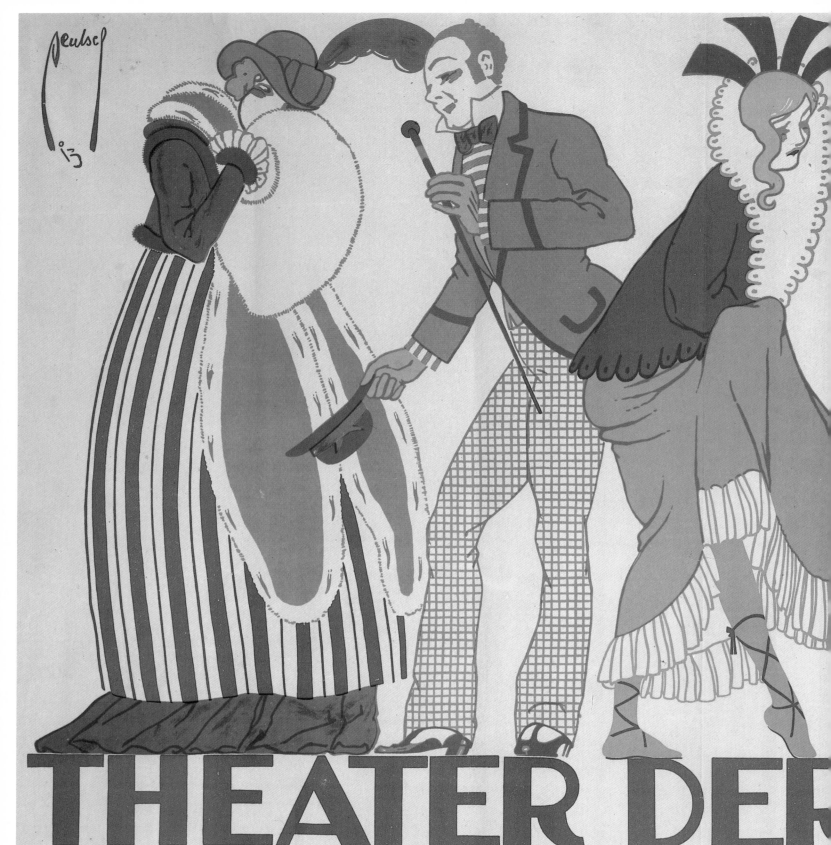

THEATER DER

MANNEQUINS VIVANTS, GR. HE

GEÖFFNET 10 UHR MORGENS - 11 UHR ABENDS

14. SEPT. - 5. OKT. 1913. AUSSTELLUN

Stone lithographic poster advertising a 'Theatre of Fashion with live models', Berlin, 1913.

Stone lithographic poster for Speck's
Orient Cinema, Zurich circa 1912.

Opposite
Stone lithographic poster featuring
actress Henny Porten in an early
German silent film, 1914.

Full-page illustration from the Viennese magazine *Elegante Welt*, 1913.

Opposite
Stone lithographic poster, featuring Asta Nielsen as star of the film *Comediens*, 1913.

Below
Stone lithographic poster, untitled but possibly for Asta Nielsen in an early German silent film circa 1913.

Asta Nielsen

"Komödianten"

von Urban Gad

Internationale
Film-Vertriebs-Gesellschaft m.b.H.
Berlin

Magazine advertisement for Manoli
Cigarettes, 1912.

Magazine advertisement for Manoli
Cigarettes, 1912.

Book cover design for *Galante Frauen*, 1917. (*Elegant Women*, a collection of ten portraits by Ernst Dryden.)

Illustration from the *Gazette du Bon Ton* which author Hans Reimann accused Dryden of plagiarising, 1913.

Illustration by Ernst Dryden from *Elegante Welt*, 1914.

Previous pages
Cover design for satirical book *Lauter Lügen* (Nothing but Lies), 1913.

Cover design for satirical book *Der Perverse Maikaefer* (The Perverse Mayfly), 1913.

Earlier English poster for pianos, which Hans Reimann also accused Dryden of copying.

Dryden's poster for Mercedes typewriters, 1911.

Plakat und Plagiat

ELEGANTE HERREN= MODEN

Szafranski 1915

Beilagen zum Aufsatze
von Hans Meyer

Meyer

Das Plakat
Juli 1915

Sebastian
Saltz d. J.

VIENNA

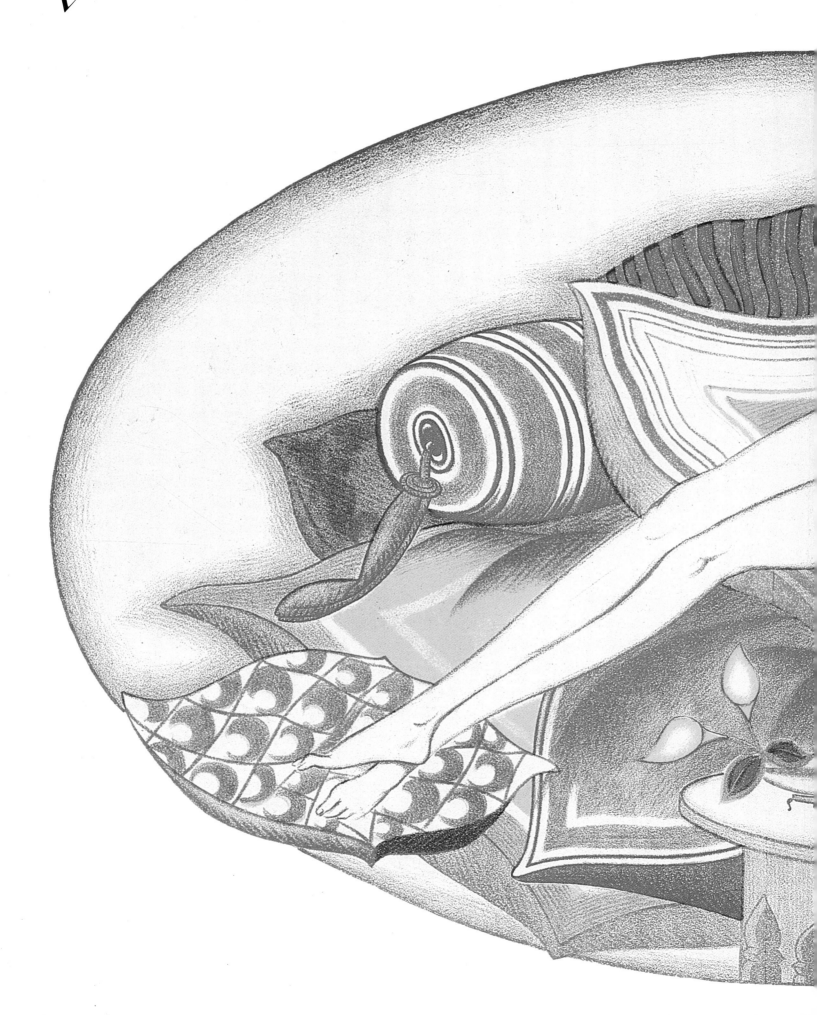

POLITICAL
CONCERNS

O N RETURNING to Austria in 1919, Dryden found a very different country from the one he had left in 1910. Nevertheless, it may also have been one to which he felt more committed, for only in this period of his career did Dryden turn his art to political use and in effect gave expression to some of his social concerns.

Vienna itself had changed. From having been the hub of Austria-Hungary, it had yet to come to terms with the overnight disposal of its Empire. It was no longer the capital of a nation of sixty million but of merely six million. It had been massively defeated in war and the Treaty of St Germain was a piece of post-war psychological oppression in itself.

Two posters from this time, one of which is housed in The Albertina Museum in Vienna – and already signed under his new name of Dryden – show him lending his art to make a political statement. In the first poster, as in most political posters – which is probably why Dryden did so few of them – there was a cumbersome written message: 'Viennese! Don't let your Granary of German South Moravia be taken away from you.' The message was a piece of defiance for a defeated nation: exhortation to the Viennese not to cede German South Moravia – its bread basket – as it was thought impossible in 1919 that a tiny landlocked nation of six million people could survive without its agricultural lands. The image that Dryden used to convey his message was strikingly powerful – a bread-knife cuts like an axe through the map of Austria which is shown as a bread-board, to illustrate the part of Austria in danger of ceding. In fact South Moravia was ceded, and subsequent history proved, contrary to what Dryden or many of his contemporaries would have believed, just how well a small country could fare in the modern economic world.

By the time of his second political poster later in the same year he seems to have perceived the new way forward too, for its subject is an advertisement for the Austrian Section of the League of Nations, depicting an idealized male youth holding the palm of peace. The message was now survival through membership and interdependence with other nation-states. It is the only extant example of a Dryden collotype print – an expensive and refined form of printing rarely used for posters. The item is sepia and in this subtler poster the message is indeed the image.

At the same time as these items were produced, Dryden may have hoped to begin his career again in the field of newspaper illustration. Both in Austria and Germany with so much political debate there was an explosion of journalism, pamphleteering and periodical writing. Karl Kraus's *Die Fackel* (The Torch) still blazed its trail, and the stalwart *Neue Freie Presse* (New Free Press), founded in 1864 and later to evolve into today's *Die Presse* (The Austrian equivalent of *The Times*), attempted to hold its head up above the divisions.

In 1919 Dryden designed several mock-ups for the front page of *Neue Freie Presse* as well as *Der Spiegel*; and in a cartoon intended for another paper or supplement called *T.W.* he drew a picture of a bound prisoner attempting to read over the top of a paper held by three hooded executioners. The alternative captions offered by Dryden read: 'You too should read *T.W.* with the respect it deserves' or 'Every week *T.W.* brings interesting reports'.

In the top right hand corner of the image is scribbled in pencil the words 'Herr Deutsch!', perhaps a wry comment on his recent past, for surely he above all knew the power of the written word.

But as the debate over the political future raged, Dryden returned to his roots

Previous page
**Illustration from a printed
advertisement for a shampoo product.**

and by 1920-21 had recovered some of his optimism. He opened a studio at No 2 Trattnerhof and took on pupils, working as never before, creating practically a factory of fashion design.

Just as Dryden himself had been a student of Klimt and the Kunstgewerbeschule, so he too became a teacher to a whole new generation of young Viennese designers – many of whom were too young to have experienced the war directly and who only knew of Dryden through the idealized pictures of his work that they had seen.

STUDIO
OF
FASHION

The first impression of the studio at Trattnerhof in the elegant centre of town was of an unusual and attractive staircase with fashion plates as exhibits on the walls, which led up to the hallway. Dryden's office was on one side – a model of his own interior decoration – and the large studio across the way contained the students who were putting into practice the master's ideas.

Wanting to be a designer in Vienna at this period was like wanting to get into television now. It was a glamorous world: in this case one that attracted because of its stylish product – elegant and serene design. And yet the real world of creativity for the offspring of Victorian-minded parents, seeking any route they could to become part of the Jazz Age, could also be something of a shock.

Trude Rachlitz, the only girl in the studio, who later became well known under the name of Ettinger as front cover illustrator and designer for the magazine *Ambassador*, found herself among a group of men that included an up-and-coming designer by the name of Fritz Lang (later to become the visionary film director of *Metropolis* but at this time more interested in fashion).

Her example was typical. Mistakenly marrying at the age of 19 she had run off to Vienna with the sole object of doing anything she could to become a designer – if at all possible with Dryden. In heavy disguise of grown-up clothes, gloves, high heels, a veil and an enormous hat she turned up on Dryden's doorstep in the hope of getting accepted. If she was accepted, it would mean not only a career, but a world of glamour, modelling, drawing, beauty, elegance. Dryden, on the other hand, seeing that under the heap of clothes was just a very young girl, lifted up the veil and told her, 'Don't try to look older than you are. If you really want to be a designer go and draw me some pictures of real life, and when you come back we'll see what we can do for you.'

Years later, when another young designer wanted to find her way into fashion and paid a visit to Dryden, who was by this time in Paris, she had a similar experience. Egon Wellesz was a famous Austrian musical director, whose portrait was painted by Kokoschka in 1911. He also had a daughter by the name of Lisi. It was she who turned up in Paris to show Dryden her drawings, expecting that the creator of the marvellous fashion plates from *Die Dame* would be as ideal as his designs. Instead she was shocked by Dryden's suggestion that it would be a good exercise for her to copy some pornographic drawings and sell them on Boulevard Montparnasse.

If this sounds unduly harsh on a young girl, it nevertheless makes the point that below the fantastical shapes of Dryden's stylized lines was an insistence on true draughtsmanship. This is what he expected of those who worked for him. Dryden's many nude sketches show that it was just as necessary to know how to draw the unclothed figure as the clothed.

With a studio full of young and energetic talent, Dryden was able to put into practice some of his grander schemes, which also included interior design

Fancy-dress party in Vienna circa 1919. Dryden is situated at the centre of the picture. On the wall is an Egger-Lienz oil painting of a First World War subject.

projects, no drawings of which now exist. But in addition to this, by having a studio at all, he was in effect espousing the young and was in touch with their wishes and needs.

With the war over, fashion now had to be created for a very different world. The generation now around him was in a sense more conscious of the liberating influence of fashion than its corseted elders. Corsets had begun to be abandoned far earlier, around 1908, but whereas then it would have been in an atmosphere of mild rebelliousness, it was now a flat rejection of the past and those who had been responsible for the war. If fashion can be said at times to reach out as the true self-expresion of an age, through garments and clothes, then the world of 1921 was badly in need of such expression.

Dryden's studio must have held out this prospect, answering directly the need that the youth of Vienna felt. For fashion made a marvellous contrast to politics, art or literature — at least fashion could change! Perhaps that is why the youth of that period, and even great artists like Fritz Lang, should have been drawn to it, as it was a way of shaping their own destiny as individuals and cutting the umbilical cord with the past. It is in the light of this need that a number of different forces came together to produce Dryden's next venture: as designer to the old-established firm of menswear tailors — Knize.

K NIZE

By 1921 Dryden's career began to develop in parallel to the fortunes of the men's tailors and outfitters firm of Knize & Co, perhaps best known as the shop that supplied Kokoschka with a number of his suits in exchange for paintings, and which still exists at their same premises at No 13 Graben, Vienna.

The story of Knize, and its illustrious development to the pinnacle of elegance and desirability is also the story of Dryden's association with it and the fortuitous relationship between three men — Fritz Wolff the owner, Dryden the designer, and Adolf Loos the architect — who together produced an unbeatable mix of talent.

Knize was established by a Czech family in 1858 in the heyday of the reign of Austrian Emperor Franz Josef. The Knize family were expert cutters, which was a solid basis for a firm of outfitters of a traditional kind, and they used to make the riding clothes for Empress Elizabeth. The Wolff family on the other hand were Berlin Jews with banking and textile interests.

In about 1880 Albert Wolff had gone on a trip around Europe in search of a business that would interest him. He had the backing of his uncle, and the trip resulted in his purchase of an interest in the Knize firm, which thus became Knize and Company. But perhaps as important as his acquisition of a percentage of Knize was his simultaneous acquisition of his Viennese Jewish wife, Gisela, whose own character and the character of her family were to be a formative influence on the future of the business.

Gisela's family name was in fact Steiner. She was the sister of Hugo Steiner, whose house in Hietzing is one of the monuments to the career of Adolf Loos, and whose daughters are recorded in sketches of two children by Egon Schiele. The Steiner family were themselves in business as suppliers of artificial flowers and hat feathers; Loos had designed the shopfront of their store Kunstblumen & Straussfedern in about 1907.

What better precursors of fashion could their combined businesses be? From *belle époque* hats and feathers to the slim elegant lines that were to become all the rage after the turn of the century. The circumstances for a remarkably creative business relationship were almost set. But soon after buying out the remaining stake in Knize in 1902, Albert Wolff died, and the prospects of the company appeared similarly shortlived as his intended heir, Fritz, was only twelve years old.

Into the breach, though, stepped a woman of vision — Gisela. Instead of winding up the business she announced she was going to keep it going for her son, with the result that from 1902 and through the First World War, the firm of men's tailors was uncharacteristically run by a woman. Not only that, but the first of its major developments was to take place — its first ever shopfront and a new interior design were created in about 1909 by Adolf Loos.

Loos's buildings, characterised by their flat roofs, accent on function, the belief in the decorativeness of the materials themselves and horror of ornament, look modern even today. In 1909 they were stunning and sometimes rejected. Emperor Franz Josef of Austria had been in residence at the Hofburg since ascending to the throne on 2 December 1848. It was said that he regarded Loos's design of the Goldmann & Salatsch building in 1911 on the Michaelerplatz opposite the palace as a personal insult, and could never bring himself to look out of the window on this side of the palace again.

On the other hand, anyone wishing to ally themselves with all that was modern, new, exciting and cosmopolitan, could not do better than employ someone like Loos. Architecture was a natural expression of this modernism. It established a link between Knize and the most forward-looking aspects of Viennese cultural life, and probably helped Knize's designs to become the most sought-after clothes in Vienna — they had the hallmark of novelty and the modern world expressed through fashion.

The structural changes which Loos effected mirrored the new step fashion was about to take. Like most tailors until this period, Knize did not have a shopfront. So, in 1902, when Gisela moved in, not exactly over the shop, but at the back of what was a long building, the main area was, and still is, on the first floor. It was regarded as more decorous not to flaunt one's wares on the High Street and this created the sense of personal attention and privacy required for the fitting of royal or aristocratic personages. Loos's first task was to create a shopfront, and by doing so he ushered the world of men's tailoring into an entirely new era.

Again the development was fortuitous, for it was only due to the fact that the bookshop next door was in financial difficulty that the tiny space for a shopfront was acquired. It was what Loos did with the space which showed his talent. Loos's father had been a stone-cutter, and this was one of the reasons he often used best marbles and natural materials in his architectural designs.

He faced the portals of Knize with black marble and created an all-glass exterior on either side of the doorway. On entering (and as very little ground floor space was purchased) the customer was faced with a delicately ranged staircase with a white linen carpet (that had to be washed twice a week) and brass runners holding it down, which led up to the spacious fitting rooms above. The walls up the staircase were of cherry-wood, as was the banister which curved in a 'U' shape up to the first floor. Carved rectangular spaces were set into the walls of the staircase to accommodate a series of prints.

Once on the first floor a series of oak panelled walls and alcoves spread out following the building in an 'L' shape with fitting rooms off the main corridor. Due to Loos's horror of wasted space he created a mezzanine where the book-keeping took place. The carpet on this floor was of green felt. The ties were stored in glass-fronted, brass-handled sliding drawers ranged like the shelves of

New letter-heading under the name *Dryden* with early version of the D logo, at this stage upper-case. Wording reads: Workshop for interior and shopfront design and exhibition stands.

A later photograph of the Knize
shopfront. The building was designed
by Adolf Loos, the Knize lettering in the
window and oval motif on the door
were designed by Dryden.

An early shop-window display circa
1925, showing definite Dryden
influence in pairing disembodied hats,
ties, scarves, cloth and shoes in
symmetrical series.

The coffered wood interior of Knize as created by Adolf Loos, showing first floor and mezzanine where the book-keepers worked. There was a hole in the mezzanine floor through which bills and receipts were passed.

The narrow ground-floor entrance to Knize showing the cherry-wood-panelled cases, some glass fronted, containing socks, ties, scarves and cloth. Note the crystal bottles of Knize cologne on the far wall as well as the wooden sculpture of the Polo player and, at the far end, the white linen-covered staircase leading to the spacious fitting rooms upstairs.

Knize Ten logo illustrated on the headed notepaper of the Paris shop at Avenue des Champs-Elysées.

Knize Ten cologne, as it was advertised in about 1926, showing the Knize lettering and logo carried through on to product and box.

a library. On first seeing the interior one gets the impression of the interior of a wooden ship with coffered ceiling, rather like Liberty's of London.

The scene was set for the arrival of Ernst Dryden and the further development of the business by Fritz Wolff. Wolff had, like Dryden, served in the First World War, becoming a lieutenant in the Cavalry. On his return from the front when hostilities ceased he duly succeeded to the management of the store in 1918. But Gisela's last and major influence on the store was still to come, for it was she who first met and appointed Dryden, thus establishing the long relationship between him and Knize.

Apparently their meeting was quite by chance for the only surviving account of it is as follows. While walking on the Ringstrasse, Mrs Wolff, who was quite a small though lively lady, had met a remarkably well-dressed man. Being in the fashion business she buttonholed him and asked, 'Where did you get such an elegant suit?' – to which Dryden replied, 'I didn't, I designed it myself.'

It sounds a wholly reasonable proposition. A glance at any photo of Ernst Dryden will show that he does stand out from the crowd wherever he is – and that his projection of himself at all times, which in anyone else could only be described as vanity, was his trademark. For Dryden indeed it was more than that: it was his livelihood and his whole life, although vanity was also an important ingredient.

Through Dryden the designer concept for men's tailors came of age. It had been tested for women's boutiques and *haute couture*, but never in menswear. It was Ernst Dryden's concept to create the designer stamp around the name of Knize and in effect merchandize the name. It was a new selling concept, utterly male, that was not taken further until the arrival of Ralph Lauren, who in turn recognizes the debt to both Dryden and Knize.

What Dryden then set about achieving for Knize was a remarkable historical first. He and Fritz Wolff together made Knize's clothes without any question the most desirable in Vienna. A suit from Knize was the fantasy of a generation of young Austrians.

In addition to the firm's established reputation, Dryden was able to offer an extra dimension which was to create this desirability. Examples of Dryden's work show how he set about this. First of all Dryden developed the Knize trademark. He had visited London shortly before and found it a most stimulating place from a fashion point of view. He was overcome with awe by the traditionalism of England, its formalities but also its materials. He was particularly impressed by Burberry and advocated that every well-dressed man should have a Burberry trenchcoat. He was particularly interested by the rules which guided English fashion and tailoring: best materials, best needlework, best cutting – in short, quality. For this is what 'English' or 'Made in England' meant. It meant certainty and something that would last.

It was perhaps with this in mind that he created a logo for Knize which was partly an imitation of an English trademark. The lettering was clear and easy to read – Loos would have undoubtedly approved – and it was stating an irrefutable fact. Dryden had seen, perhaps before anyone else on the continent, that the way the English sold was in a sense by appearing not to sell. They did not advertise excessively, but when it was stated 'Shirtmakers to the King', they really were, or when they said Established 1850, 1750 or earlier this was unsurprising and true.

The under-selling technique, the belief that the company's honour and reputation were staked jointly and severally on every item bearing the company's

Portrait photograph by Man Ray of actor Adolphe Menjou in relaxed Knize attire, Paris, 1930.

mark and stamp – this Dryden was to incorporate into the logo of Knize. Transferred into the context of Vienna, the logo became not an understatement but a striking selling point by way of its novelty and truly un-Austrian approach.

It was probably partly inspired by the logo of James Lock & Co Ltd, Hatters of Jermyn Street, whose mark today is still black lettering on a white oval background. Lock's logo does not look particularly remarkable in an English context, but transferred to Vienna, the style, even the lettering, seemed strange, modern and un-German in origin. Thus the creation of the Knize mark was Dryden's first contribution to the Knize image.

But Dryden's work went far beyond this. The mark had to mean what it said, just as it did in England, and Dryden with his inimitable classic elegance designed suits and examples of how the suits would look when worn. He designed the Knize leaflet in all its simplicity and directness, and then with Fritz Wolff developed a range of men's toiletries such as had never been seen before in male fashion – soaps, toilet water, talcs, perfume, hair-lotions, brilliantine, shaving cream, shaving soap, bearing the mark, some in bottles of ground crystal. For women there was even a sun-tan oil. It was Gucci before Gucci and Polo before Ralph Lauren. This was literally the case. As the lines developed stage by stage, Dryden and Wolff took the British sport of nobles and cavalrymen – polo – as a symbol of elegance and long before Ralph Lauren formed his company, whose whole existence is based on this concept, Knize produced a line called *Polo Ten*, ten being the highest handicap in polo. This is the origin of the current Knize – 'Ten' range of products and toiletries.

Then, with Loos as architect and Dryden as designer, Fritz Wolff was ready to expand the Knize concept and, in a way that has been repeated by other firms many times since but which was new then, he opened other Knize stores: in Karlsbad in 1921, Berlin in 1924, Paris in 1928, Prague in the early 1930s (which became a *cause célèbre* between the now small country of Austria versus the new Czech Republic who regarded the opening as a threat to the Czech cutter's industry), Bad Gastein in 1937; other stores followed later after Dryden's death.

A life-size polo player on his horse was constructed in plaster and placed within the luxurious marble building of the Paris store at 146 Avenue des Champs-Elysées. Through Dryden the mark of Knize became transferable, saleable and desirable in other markets, the breakthrough that is sought by every leading fashion designer today.

Perhaps no one could have been better suited to this task than Dryden, because his talents for promotion and his skill in actual design were perfectly complementary in this venture. One of the main achievements of Dryden's career is to have been the forerunner of a type of promotion that has only been fully exploited with the greater communication available in the present day. Knize, on its existing premises on the Graben, still sports Dryden's trademark on its toiletries over fifty years after it was designed. But with the loss of Fritz Wolff's business skills – he died in New York in 1949 – and the ravages of the war, the firm slowly retracted.

More importantly, fashion moved on, something Dryden and Gisela Wolff understood, although the wheel can almost be said to have turned full circle today with the renewed interest in male fashion and the success of the firm of Ralph Lauren. Apart from all of Dryden's other achievements, he was one of the finest menswear designers of the 1920s, and his designs for men are some of the very few excellent drawings in this genre that exist.

Hello

The three sisters, (left to right) Hello, Fritzi, and Lily circa 1912, wearing dresses made by Marianne whom Hello later employed as her seamstress, and bottom, Hello in 1922, around the time she met Dryden.

The story of Hello and the creation of her boutique of the same name is one of the unbroken threads which runs through the life of Ernst Dryden. Hello, who was never called by her real name 'Helene', was the youngest of three sisters, born at exactly the turn of the century. She was in a sense the true spirit of Vienna 1900 and was to become Dryden's business associate and to remain his lifelong friend.

Her parents (my great grandparents), Ferdinand and Emma Krasa, originally came from Prague and it was her father who called his youngest 'Hello', thus dubbing her with a name and character which partly made her what she became – a headstrong young lady who wanted to work in the world of fashion and would settle for nothing else. Her upbringing had been sheltered from the horrors of the First World War. The world she had grown up in still consisted of summers spent by the Austrian lake town of Bad Ischl, where the Emperor stayed, or by the Wolfgangsee. Her parents were indulgent and liberal.

It was not surprising, therefore, that the young Hello should wish to be a part of the world of Vienna that opened up before her – the movements in art, literature and psycho-analysis all of which made Vienna, in spite of the war, a most exciting place in which to live. Certainly, Hello had no dreams of staying at home but was one of a number of women who wanted to go out and earn a living. And so it was that in about 1920 Hello met and married a young lieutenant, fresh from his army service, Fritz Wolff, the owner of Knize, and by doing so married into fashion. What she didn't know was that within a year Ernst Dryden was to appear on the scene and that when he did he would so captivate her that it would end this marriage very shortly afterwards.

It seems that Dryden needed to find someone like Hello. After the break-up of his first marriage he had vowed never to marry again, and throughout his relationship with Hello there was never any question of marriage. To Dryden she was something else – she was representative of her age, the ideal of the liberated and working woman, and through her he seemed to find a way to express his feelings for the new way in which fashion would develop.

Dryden continued to receive commissions from Knize while together they created from small beginnings a fashion business which they called Hello and into which they both channelled enormous efforts; so much so that by 1936 it was the most successful women's dressmaker in Vienna. For Dryden it was also an opportunity to develop a separate business from scratch, to create a fashion concept after his own image. It was not enough for him to be working on only one project. In Hello he seems to have found a foil for his own creativity. If her wish to enter the fashion world was insatiable, his creativity was fuel for the fire.

After her parting from Fritz Wolff, the first steps were taken with Dryden's help. With money scarce in the aftermath of the First World War the aristocracy was hard-up and had to think of inventive ways of working or raising money. This prompted Dryden to effect an introduction for Hello to Countess Wydenbruck, whose house at No 3 Gusshausstrasse was too large for her requirements and possibly too expensive to maintain.

The Countess took to Hello immediately and rented rooms to her. It was a perfect formula. Dryden would supply her with designs, and the Countess's social circle would provide the clientele. The business was almost ready to take shape.

An essential part of any dress-making business, however, is an expert cutter. In the Krasa family there had always been a Czech seamstress called Marianne,

The Hello shopfront, Graben 14,
Vienna, 1936, showing a Dryden design
in the window. Designed by Baumfeld,
the father of one of Hello's assistants,
the shopfront was made entirely out of
marble and glass.

Design in pencil and wash for an
overcoat, with 'd' signature and Hello
lettering, epitomising the outdoor
sporty look she specialised in circa
1936.

The greyhound motif for Hello's shop
on the Graben which opened in 1936.

who had made the three girls' frocks and tunics throughout their childhood. With the youngest, Hello, now gone she was out of service. Hello therefore hauled Marianne out of her family home to come and work for her. Now the picture was complete.

The story of the growth of Hello as a dressmaker is based on this fortuitous mix of elements founded on the energy and taste of Hello and the direction of Dryden. As with Knize and before at Kersten & Tuteur, Dryden focused the idea of the firm into an image. Hello, as a name, signified a bright and modern fashion concept. Sounding like an English greeting, it was inviting and fulfilled the Continental craving for things American and English.

To match this, the Hello lettering was kept simple and legible. And one form of it was devised through an imitation of personal handwriting (something that has only recently come back into fashion amongst modern designers and typesetters fed up with impersonal standard typefaces). In Dryden's case at this time it was the wish to breathe fresh air into the image and make it stand out from the gothic script commonly used by other stores. Finally, to complete the image, a display advertisement incorporated a standard poodle as the fashion motif.

Soon the one rented room became three or four, and the business flourished. The progress of their love affair and business relationship is recorded in their correspondence, which was to continue without interruption over the next seventeen years. In an early letter we can see how the difference in age was a factor in their relationship. For Dryden, the First World War was still very fresh in the memory. In 1923 he wrote on a postcard sent from Italy:

Remembering blessed Toni, have just left a bunch of Edelweiss in a war cemetery.
Very affectionately, yours Ernst.

Towards the end of the war Dryden had been posted as recorder of flight movements to the Isonzo front line with Italy, where fighting was worst and here, as in many other letters, we see the other side of the man whose designs on first sight sometimes appear to reflect so little of the turmoils of the century.

Hello seems to have kept all Dryden's letters and re-read them. There are many photographs of the couple together, collected in albums. Pictures of them at winter escapes, or later by the sea or in his car. The letters record not only Dryden's relationship with Hello but, as the letter headings change, also his steps across Europe. He also writes to her from hotels when he is away on buying trips to London or Berlin.

On one such trip to London in the later 1920s he wrote to her from the Park Lane Hotel, Piccadilly:

Dearest Child,
Everything here is like this notepaper; this is why you should come here once a year. It is the best, the most stable, the most beautiful place in the world. A walk down Piccadilly gives you courage, a visit to Fortnum & Mason's, Swaine Adeney & Brigg is itself an event! These people have style, bearing and an unshakeable confidence. Only they and the French count. There is no sign of crisis here, the Continental insolence never existed, nor the provocative conduct of the petits bourgeois. And then this 'to be English!' Not at all like the false and deceitful Germanism.

We are enjoying a thousand different things, we delight in the feeling of empathy with many aspects of life here. I might be very successful here as a

Dryden and Hello together on holiday in the late 1920s.

Following page
Dryden at the wheel of his Austro-Daimler circa 1923. Dryden designed the bodywork himself. In the back wearing glasses is Hello.

Top **Portrait of model sporting a Hello jacket designed by Dryden. The photographer was Dora Kallmus, Paris, 1936.**

Bottom **A contemporary photograph of the interior of Hello's shop on the Graben circa 1936, showing Dryden's designs on the right and Hello wrapping paper on the counter.**

creator of fashion, as a dressmaker, because many things are rather odd. I will have to think about it. The only drawback is the climate. Everything else is fine. The country life, the link with the world, six hours travel from Paris!

Through Dryden, Hello's eyes were being widened to broader horizons. He showed her how her shop, even in its Viennese context, could profit by influences from abroad. And consistent with their difference in age he does not write to her 'my darling' or 'my love' – but 'my child', 'my Hello-child', 'my boy'.

The 'little boy' nicknames stemmed from her boyish looks and her somewhat serious expression, which belied her mischievousness and humour. Her boyishness was also her chic. It was the chic of the age. Gender was indeterminate. Boyishness in fashion added a frisson of sexual excitement. Time and again in his designs Dryden later used her features as the model for his most stylish women, and in those designs she became slimmer and taller than she in fact was.

As the letters progress they record Dryden's move in 1926 to Paris, the growing unrest in Europe, the difficulties of getting fabrics. Without Dryden to guide her, her business appears to run into innumerable difficulties, which vicariously cause him endless sleepless nights. And yet the business at the same time seems erratically to be succeeding.

His affair with Hello, odd and complicated as it was, was almost certainly initiated by Hello. In an early letter that Hello may have had good reason to keep he wrote: 'You were very naughty last night, there is serious danger when children come to see one. Not very pedagogic! However we shall try.'

She could also be a lady of moods and temper. From one of his early addresses, No 2 Metternichgasse, Dryden wrote to her with mock-humility: 'I hope Dear Lady you are not only free from pain but in a better mood. If I can serve you in any way, you know I am at your service . . .'

Later, when Dryden left for Paris, his letters were filled with choice pieces of information for the next season's fashion, advice on where to obtain materials, exhorting her to work harder and promising holidays together later. By 1936 Hello was ready to move from Gusshausstrasse. She purchased a building in the most fashionable district of Vienna at No 14 Graben, by coincidence exactly opposite Knize.

This must surely have been the pinnacle of Hello's achievement. The architectural design of the shopfront was an all glass affair with marble surround, stunning in its simplicity, which would look as chic and modern today as when it was built in 1936. The architect was Baumfeld, father of one of Hello's assistants. Perhaps to signify the move up-market, the poodle motif from Gusshausstrasse became a greyhound.

Among her first customers at the new premises were the Duke and Duchess of Windsor, who at that time were staying at the small Austrian resort of Enzesfeld near Vienna. It is perhaps characteristic of Hello that on this occasion at the very height of her success she was overcome with stagefright and, nervous of her poor English, she went swimming, leaving her manageress to handle the visit.

However, as war approached, Dryden who was by now in Hollywood, was writing to her with great foreboding about the future. As her business appeared to be doing so well, it is not surprising that she appeared unwilling to give it up and move. Even Dryden, who had been so tough with himself, was not as insistent with her as he might have been. One of his latest extant letters, written on headed notepaper from the Garden of Allah Hotel, gives an indication of his fears:

My dearest Hellochild,

Thank you for the somewhat happier Easter letter. The so-called political situation! Yes, that is it. However, I have foreseen this since 1925 and I have little hope that it will ever recover. What to do? Only, carry on and build up the business as much as possible in order to sell it one day, just before you depart for Moscow or Hollywood.

'Sell' is not really the right word, because in your part of the world that is no longer even possible; perhaps to exchange it for a small apartment block if this is still possible, which is also doubtful. The situation is not surprising and one must look at it realistically.

The ones who have stayed behind have all shown great courage because it was much simpler to run away as I have done.

The letter was written on 15 April 1936 and shows how, away from the difficulties in Europe, he is even starting to criticize himself for leaving. The letter continues with other advice: perhaps a branch in Prague would be safe? 'If Hello opens up in Prague I would go to New York myself and pack five cases of "opening" stuff and the people in Prague will just gape.' But it was not to be: 'Hellochild,' he wrote, 'just carry on. Nothing will happen to us. We have so much more than millions of people. We have ourselves.'

When Dryden died a few years later Hello was still in Vienna. By this time she had indeed sold the business, one of the last to be able to do so, and she was finally on the point of taking Dryden's advice. On 1 December 1938, almost nine months after his death, *Women's Wear Daily* reported as follows:

Hello Wolff – Budischowsky, head of 'Hello' Graben, Viennese creator of sports models and accessories, has left Vienna for London.

Without her motivation and Dryden's designs the store did not continue after the war. In London she started her business again from an address at Manchester Square and then at Bruton Street. Her devotion to fashion never faded. Even after her London business had finally closed, and although she was already in her early seventies, she took a job as a sales assistant on the perfume counter of Harrods, just to be near the world she loved. It used to cost her more money to get there than she earned.

Her devotion to the memory of Dryden never faded either. In her life she had been married four times – but her one great love was the man she never married. His letters were all preserved, and one section, mainly his letters from Hollywood, were even kept in a ring folder to be read and re-read. And it is because his designs were sent to her from Hollywood after his death that we are able to appreciate Dryden's works today.

Stone lithographic poster with a
political message, 1919.

Cartoon for the periodical *TW Review*
in pencil and ink circa 1919. Written
in the top right-hand corner of
the original are the wry words
'Herr Deutsch!'.

Collotype printed poster in sepia tone
for The Austrian Section of the League
of Nations, 1919.

THEATRE ART EXHIBITION

LONDON 1924

Opposite
Partly stencilled design for an advertisement for a Theatre Art Exhibition, London, 1924.

Cubist-style design in crayon and pencil of a woman circa 1923.

Part of a series of pencil sketches of
erotica circa 1926 onwards.

Stage design in crayon showing candlelit dinner for twenty-three circa 1920.

Opposite
Stone lithographic poster for a film entitled *The Secrets of Paris* circa 1921.

Original luggage labels designed by Dryden, *de rigueur* in a new age of fashionable travelling.

Stone lithographic poster advertising a Fashion Grand Prix on June 20th, 1920.

Stone lithographic poster advertising the type of natural dance performance beloved of this era circa 1921. Toni Birkmeyer was one of its finest exponents.

Stone lithographic poster advertising Bauer's Exquisite Liqueurs circa 1921.

Design for a display advertisement in pencil and wash for Knize circa 1928.

Four shoe designs in pencil and wash which were actually executed for French menswear magazine *Adam*, but which could easily have been appropriate to Knize at that time circa 1928.

Design in gouache and pencil for smart male afternoon wear. Note the foulard in breast pocket and co-respondent shoes.

Design in gouache and pencil for
skating wear circa 1928.

Design for the keen racer.

Evening-wear design for
the man at his club
or out to dinner.

Design in gouache and pencil for a
morning suit epitomising the Knize man
circa 1928.

Design in gouache for lightweight
mackintosh and spats circa 1928.

↑HE LOST WORLD OF DIE DAME

D I E D A M E magazine today is little known and even more rarely discussed. And yet, for a certain generation of Germans and Austrians, those two words symbolized all that was stylish, elegant and modern in the world of fashion. Founded in 1912 by the Ullstein family, whose publishing empire included several Berlin newspapers and a host of small publishing off-shoots, *Die Dame* was intended to strike upwards into the highest echelons of the market and almost be an art object in itself. It was unashamedly elitist.

Condé Nast had only bought *Vogue* in the United States three years earlier, so it was a parallel rather than imitative development. *Die Dame's* differences from *Vogue* were as important as its similarities. Right from the beginning it had something of a literary and intellectual slant that *Vogue* never really allowed itself, and later in its heyday of the 1920s and 30s, when *haute couture* was at its height, *Die Dame* could be far more earthy if it wanted to. Part of this was due to the different structure of *Die Dame*, the character of its owners and editors and the character of Germany. Seriousness was never held to be a huge virtue in France or the US and readers there would have been more put off by the thoughtful articles on painters, philosophers, theatre directors and writers which so regularly appeared in *Die Dame*.

In historical terms *Die Dame* appears enormously interesting, because it effectively records not how Germany was – but how it might have been. It shows the many creative threads of talent in the arts, of which some were soon to be smothered for ever and others were to emerge later in the context of Hollywood. Whole speeches given by Max Reinhardt, the grand director of German versions of Shakespeare, were reprinted. We see actors who while known to all Germany, we may know only from small bit parts from Hollywood – such as Conrad Veidt – dancers such as Lena Amsel and Tilly Losch. Painters whose studios were visited included Max Pechstein, George Grosz and Willy Jaeckel. Writers whose works were serialized or premiered included André Maurois, Colette (who also wrote many pieces for *Vogue*) and Stefan Zweig.

But *Die Dame's* difference from *Vogue* of the same period lay perhaps in its range. At one and the same time it could observe and comment on what was newest in fashion from the streets of Paris and yet also include extraordinarily risqué photographs under the cover of art which would have made its French sister blush to see. Perhaps a good example of this is the photograph of a so-called Japanese Noh-dancer, a stunningly erotic piece whose subject would be more likely to be found in a Berlin night-spot than in any Noh play.

In its day *Die Dame* sold on average about 60,000 copies per issue and sometimes appeared twice a month. It made lavish use of colour, it was never cheap and it was never snobbish either. It was elitist rather than snobbish, for in the *Die Dame* scale of values it was not money or class that counted but talent, wherever that talent might truly be found – whether it be in the arts or business. Its values were rather like those in the story of the American lady who let it be known she was to arrive at the Kaiser's party in a dress that had cost her 50,000 marks – and promptly had her invitation withdrawn; while the couturier who created her dress was made a welcome guest.

Dryden would have been aware of *Die Dame's* development in Berlin from as early as 1912 when it was founded. But at that time the front covers that he was designing were for another purely fashion magazine, *Elegante Welt*. By the time Dryden began to work for *Die Dame* it had already been going for fourteen

Japanese Noh dancer and typical page from *Die Dame* in terms of artistic daring.

Previous page
Detail taken from the published front cover of *Die Dame* illustrating a woman in driving gear in front of her Bugatti, 1930.

years and was a part of Berlin life. The Ullsteins, for their part, would have known of Dryden's previous work in Berlin and Vienna. Dryden's association with *Die Dame* began in 1926 and was to last for seven years. During this time he executed on a purely freelance basis innumerable front cover designs, illustrations, occasional written pieces and sometimes even advertisements. There are issues which are dominated by his talent.

A further significant fact is that while published editions have been largely lost due to the war, through the preservation of Dryden's designs, some of the original artwork for its greatest front covers and illustrations have survived. That they were transported first out to the United States of America with Dryden's possessions in 1933 and returned to England in 1938 was one of the remarkable quirks of fate which have helped Dryden's work as a whole to be preserved: had they remained in Europe they too would most likely have been lost. As a result it is from these original gouache or pencil and watercolour designs that the illustrations in this book have been produced. Even *Vogue*, whose history is far better catalogued, is rarely able to enjoy the luxury of drawing on original artwork for its retrospective editions.

Photograph depicting the head office of one of Ullstein's newspapers, the *Berliner Morgenpost*, 1924.

Moreover, now that the role of the commercial illustrator in the 1920s and 1930s is more fully appreciated, it is possible to see the artwork for many of Dryden's *Die Dame* designs as true compositions worthy of the accolades normally accorded to art and artists of the mainstream. Although never thought of in their own day as material for exhibitions or works of art in their own right, they deserve to be looked upon now as such, however narrow their original purposes.

Two of his most exciting pieces of this kind are most probably the items depicting the fashionable woman holding up a birdcage, from which is released the new season's fashion. Through this image he has created a timeless and exciting picture. As a front cover to a magazine — one of them was used in an issue for October 1929 — it conveys perfectly and with humour the thrill of the release of a new season's fashion. Today, when the season is less structured or rigid, it is perhaps difficult to imagine how hard the fashion houses worked to clothe their new designs with secrecy or to describe the excitement with which a new design was awaited. We have to use our imagination, too, to appreciate the visual impact of the magazine, whether seen at a Berlin bookstall or lying casually on the coffee table of a rich person's house.

It is an image to make the heart leap, like the sight of a tropical bird, ensnared, but suddenly set free. Seen this way, how perfectly it captures the mood of a generation. For this is how many women felt. This indeed was the root power of fashion. While new fashions were explored and renewed with each season, the woman herself explored this freedom. It was no longer by 1926 just a freedom from the literal restrictions of hoops and corsets. That had been achieved. The proud and well-dressed lady was now defining herself in a new way in society. In a sense fashion was a most powerful expression of social freedom, and that is why these images created by Ernst Dryden for those specific issues may remain both of their period and timeless.

But before moving on, it would be wrong to overlook just how Dryden may have arrived at the specific motif of the little lady — an image which with all the rivalry and imitation in the fashion business remains proudly unique to Dryden's oeuvre and frame of mind. It is itself a kind of fashion joke. For the little lady is like the small maquette or miniature model which both artists and dressmakers use in their work to create designs in miniature. Quite simply, Dryden brings this model to life and she becomes the spirit of fashion; it is as if the little model has a mind of her own and tells the designer at his desk or drawing board what to make for her. He then releases his creation into the wind. It would be hard to find a more reasonant or pleasing image of fashion of the 1920s and 1930s.

During all this time Dryden was living and working in Paris, first from a house at 8 Rue Borghese, and later 30 Rue Peronnet — both in the fashionable western suburb of Neuilly. *Die Dame* had wanted someone at the centre of *haute couture*. Not just a journalist or a writer but something Dryden would not have called himself — an artistic journalist. In part this became just one of his many functions. For a German magazine based and printed in Berlin, Dryden's position in Paris was pivotal. As cosmopolitan as he was and yet also aware of the specific conditions of Berlin he was invaluable. But there was one even greater advantage which Dryden offered to the house of Ullstein. According to Frederick Ullstein, son of its founder, Dryden was able to enter where the journalists or artists of other magazines were often barred.

So secretive were some of the great houses of fashion in this period, such as Chanel, Worth or Patou, that neither artists with sketchbooks nor photographers with cameras were allowed into their first showings. Dryden, as a designer, one who had even designed for Chanel personally, the creator of designs in his own right, was allowed within the hallowed walls. Furthermore, Dryden was able with little difficulty to memorize designs and execute technically exact drawings later. These drawings, which may now appear to be artistically routine, had great impact when first seen in *Die Dame*, and represented some of his most valuable work in his own day. For Dryden only needed to see a design once, the way a dress hung, in order to know where the seam would need to be. When drawn, these designs were taken with utmost confidentiality by hand straight to Berlin and ready for printing.

As *haute couture* began to reach the masses via the magazines, women not only wanted to see the idealized versions of how designs would look when worn but also hints of how to make them up. If they could imitate a Patou or Molyneaux design rather than buy the real thing, most were happy. Only the richest could really wear the designer label.

The reaction of the fashion houses who allowed Dryden in was ambivalent. They would have liked to bar the door to him, but could not do so as he had done nothing wrong; moreover they were flattered by the publicity and attention their designs would receive.

All this time Paris was there to be enjoyed, and as before Dryden drew on real life as his ultimate inspiration. The definition of chic had changed from the ideals he had created in Berlin. The *Die Dame* woman became an extension of the woman Dryden actually designed for. She was particular, a little haughty, self-possessed, businesslike. She took herself seriously. She also had to have vanity. He himself, we know, had vanity, the vanity to wish to be immaculately dressed and to have himself photographed looking so. The woman's vanity was conveyed by her bearing and the slant of her head. How many times Dryden, as dress designer, must have seen a woman preening herself or looking into her powder compact to make sure her make-up was perfect and hat in place.

The cover for a November issue of *Die Dame* captures this woman perfectly. It is a pastel and charcoal drawing of beautiful arrogant chic. The lady in fur wrap looks into her powder compact not surreptitiously but in self-admiration — not inquiring as to whether her appearance is perfect, but confirming that it is. Rather than seeing her hands adjusting her hat, we see her kid gloves. We do not see the pupils of her eyes, which do not look at us, but their languid lids, high eyebrows and darkened eyelashes. Above all, the lady does not smile.

On another level the picture is also a portrait of a person Dryden knew very well – for it is made up of the features of Hello. It is her face that he has idealized; it is her action of looking into the powder compact – something even I myself saw her do well into her later years. And although Hello was one of the most vital and exciting people one could ever meet, out of the many photos which remain of her, only in very few does she smile. The Dryden woman was no longer a vamp, she would be seen not at nightclubs, bars, dance tournaments, but with her chauffeur, out sporting with her man (if she chose), but above all starting to indulge in the great anthropological event of the century – shopping.

The observations of woman as consumer are depicted with some bitter-sweetness. Yet Dryden had made the link between money, purchasing power and fashion, whose force could today almost be described as one of the last great laws of nature.

Dryden in a sense designed his woman to conform to the proportions he most respected in other areas of style. The long thin legs of the ladies wearing lime greens and yellows on the cover of the issue for March 1928 are sleek like race-horses. The woman in an arena surrounded by sixteen beautiful cars instead of a car in the middle admired by sixteen women is a wonderful quip. In the picture of the woman and her husband inspecting a car show, the man is frowning at the price while the lady inwardly glows in satisfaction that the purse will be made to stretch to this beautiful object. Woman and object are one, united in elegance and style. Sometimes difficult to tell apart – and both expensive.

Today, the relationship described above is no longer a truth, but it was then. There was another truth – an observation which Dryden must have noted many times from the boulevards of Paris – that the men were inevitably much older than the women. On one level this was the inevitable attraction to riches and wealth – the stereotype of the sugar-daddy which has been often mocked – but which has its basis in a simple, harsh fact – the decimation of male youth in the First World War. There simply were not the young men around. The women who danced together at jazz parties, who wore their hair in a boyish manner, lacked men and needed to make up for it. All this was the *Die Dame* woman.

Paris itself also had a magnetic fascination for Germans. A few years later Hitler in his own macabre tribute withheld from flattening it. A poster Dryden himself had designed from Vienna in about 1920 was for the successful film *The Secrets of Paris*. Dryden, when depicting scenes with his critical and observant eye, which was intended as light relief for the magazine, drew on this fascination. He knew that the Germans as a whole only a few years after the end of the First World War were isolated; that they would dearly have wished to travel more but that neither were they generally wealthy enough or for that matter welcome. Through *Die Dame*, many Germans who could not afford to leave their country glimpsed the world. It was a world that consisted of travel, sports, shopping, café life, dancing, art appreciation, theatre. Out of all these travel had an enormous appeal. In those days a whole season was geared to it. The month of August was actually called the travelling season, conjuring up images of the real Orient Express as it once was and ocean-going liners against whose hand-rails the elegantly clad would prop themselves.

Photograph of Dryden with pet Bedlington dog at the height of his stay in Paris circa 1928.

Dryden's method of artistic reportage was to depict these scenes in caricature manner but in a way which was true to life. The pictures are often captioned by him. He depicts the life inside the coffee houses, walking in the Bois de Boulogne, being seen at art galleries. The titles of some of his occasional written pieces are as follows: 'Words overheard at breakfast in St Moritz', 'Travels by car', 'Mature and eligible gentlemen for the real lady'. In the latter piece, which filled a page of the magazine, Dryden executed five sketches of leading eligible gentlemen in London in 1929. They included Lord Lonsdale (the most popular sportsman in England, and racehorse owner), the Aga Khan, Mr E. Berry Wall, Admiral Earl Jellicoe and General Elkington. Certainly there were few young bones amongst this sample.

Although the world of fashion design was predominantly female, Dryden had been and still was equally interested in male fashions. In another illustrated article entitled 'The Gentleman in Autumn' from 1929, he made the following recommendation:

We must discard prejudice . . . I am convinced the beard is striding into fashion. Maybe we have been clean shaven for too long? . . . It makes one think of unruliness and a revolutionary way of thinking. So I am wearing one as well . . .'

The piece Dryden wrote and illustrated entitled *Dryden as adviser on Christmas presents* is an interesting record of his amusing tastes and some of the tastes of the period. In the days when it was not considered unusual to give dogs as presents he particularly recommends the Bedlington terrier. Dryden had one of his own in Paris. It was apparently not the most intelligent animal and yet in its own way, looking rather like an underfed lamb, it was incredibly chic. Apart from the study of women *Die Dame* provided Dryden with the opportunity to draw cars and dogs, and sometimes all three together. This combination was one of the ultimate formulae for elegance, as the *Die Dame* cover with woman and dog in front of a Bugatti shows.

During all this time, photography as it then was, could rub shoulders with the illustrator's art without fear of conflict. In *Die Dame* could be seen many examples of the work of another Viennese, D'Ora, who had also moved to Paris and set up a photographic studio. Dora Kallmus, as her real name was, had photographed the costume and dress design of the Wiener Werkstatte, the famous Viennese institution formed to promote Arts and Crafts. Her name crops up time and again as portrait illustrator of the famous of Vienna – lasting portraits of Karl Kraus and Alma Mahler among them.

Her pictures reveal another aspect to *Die Dame* of this period. Seen side by side with the work of *Die Dame's* illustrators there was no conflict. The photographer's art was quite simply a different way of seeing. The one did not need to exclude the other. Other photographers included E.O. Hoppé, whose photographs were given full-page scope so they might often be viewed as art themselves. The spacious lay-out, meanwhile, was intended to give images room to breathe and to convey the sense of luxury that was required.

When *Die Dame* closed in 1943 it had remained largely unchanged in format throughout its 32 years of production. It had never developed into the type of modern magazine *Vogue* became, and it remains today a proud piece of German history. If it has been largely forgotten that is perhaps because so few copies of it exist. And yet, through the work of Dryden, some of its finest drawings for covers and designs may still be enjoyed.

At the same time as designing for *Die Dame*, Dryden had a unique position with his publishers, Ullstein, for they allowed him to accept numerous outside commissions for full-page magazine advertisements. Some appeared not only in *Die Dame*, but also in French *Vogue*, particularly those for the up-and-coming couture house of Jane Regny for whom he started designing as early as 1926.

His advertising at this time reveals Dryden's ability to adapt to yet another medium, a change that some other of the Berlin poster artists were never able to make. Ludwig Hohlwein, for example, continued to plough the same furrow of poster art against all trends, finding in the end that, as the range of buyers was reduced, the only paymaster became the Third Reich.

Just as poster art had indeed been the mass media of its day, so full-page magazine advertising by 1926 had become its equivalent. New printing techniques had led to a dramatic expansion in magazine production between the wars. But magazines also had the advantage of segmenting the market — defining their appeal and therefore speaking directly to their own chosen audience. For the commercial interests who paid for such advertisements they had a ready-made context in which to sell their product or to establish its profile. With less competition too than today, the pre-eminence of *Vogue*, *Die Dame* or *Harper's* within the field of fashion meant that the choice of how to spend one's limited advertising budget was less agonizing than it would be today.

It is from this period that Dryden designed his famous three Bugatti advertisements — three of the very few ever to exist, as Ettore Bugatti was opposed to advertising in general, considering his vehicle itself to be its best advertisement. For Dryden, an automobile enthusiast himself, the urge to create a Bugatti advertisement must have been irresistible, and his Bugatti advertisements are infused with reverence for a machine that came closest to being the mechanical equivalent of one of his female models.

Everything about a Bugatti made it not just a conveyance but more a piece of motorized sculpture, and Dryden had no difficulty in conveying this through his art. For Ettore, the symbol of the vehicle was the thoroughbred, the racehorses that he loved, and his automobiles were intended to be as sleek and well trained as nature's masterpiece. For such a vehicle to be advertised within the pages of French *Vogue* or *Die Dame* was for one form of elegance to be set off by another. Dryden parodies this in one of his designs with deliberately ambiguous text and imagery:

Elle est le pur sang de la route	She is the thoroughbred of the road
Elle est la merveille de notre époque	She is the wonder of our age
Elle est une Bugatti!	She is a Bugatti!

With the slim tall figure of the fashionable woman prominent in the design, Dryden describes the car as if it had all the attributes of an elegant and thoroughbred woman.

In the blue Bugatti advertisement the use of one colour, the Bugatti blue, is a masterstroke. Firstly, it was a simplicity that would be appreciated by the printer but also the special cobalt blue colour communicated one of the effective hallmarks of a Bugatti. Etched out of this marvellous colour, the symbolic vehicles are depicted in white, inter-connected with the lower-case letters which spell the magic word — Bugatti.

*M*AGAZINE
ADVERTISING

In effect, the advertisement is a perfect application of the principles of Bauhaus styling. It was the Bauhaus that had prescribed the abolition of upper-case lettering and which strove in advertising for the communication of message via the use of shades of colour, and the reduction of an image to its essential elements rather than Art Nouveau type ornament. With tongue in cheek Dryden creates the perfect Bauhaus advertisement which would put him at the top of Kandinsky's class.

The advertisement entitled *Le Champion du Monde 1926* refers to the year in which Bugatti triumphed in the Spanish Grand Prix and won the World Championship. It shows a Type 35 Grand Prix Bugatti in racing colours, and the driver helmet-less, as was often the case. The drawing of the vehicle is perfectly accurate, right down to the handbrake, the horseshoe radiator, and the leather thongs which hold down the bonnet. Again, with economy of colour, Dryden depicts the excitement of the vehicle as it was perceived in his day – the hottest thing on four wheels in 1926.

This classic advertisement is the perfect expression of its age. It is defined by its date as a particular moment in history and speaks to us now of the smell of the race track and engine oil, of those Brooklands days which no amount of design ·could recreate now. The design is of its period and at the same time expresses its period. The lettering of the word Bugatti itself, with the letter 'G' interwoven with the wheel, exudes speed. The streamlining in yellow is purest art deco, machine-age elegance, the driver at the wheel intentionally hunched almost like a jockey at the winning-post on a thoroughbred horse. If I had to choose a single Dryden advertisement which summed up his achievements in this field it would probably be this one.

If all this sounds too idealistic a view of everyday life in the late 1920s, and an escapist vision of the period, as indeed it is meant to be, we can look for a moment at another side to those times. For in real life a Bugatti, like any car, could also be a lethal instrument. At almost the same time as Dryden completed the Bugatti series he was to write to Hello of an accident involving a Bugatti and some people he loved.

Dryden, Paris-Neuilly, 30 Rue Perronet
Tuesday

I have just been to Montparnasse and La Serre, who loved Lena dearly, he was very close to her for one year, gave an account of the catastrophe. The famous painter Derain has a property near Fontainebleau; he invited Lena and another woman (who no one was acquainted with but who was delightful, sweet, intelligent and charming, only her name Florence was known) to lunch on Sunday. Derain went ahead in his own car, while Lena and Florence followed in the Bugatti. When they did not arrive Derain eventually turned back, only to find the Bugatti enveloped in flames. La Serre, almost deranged with despair at the thought that the women might have been burned alive, went back twice to reconstruct the incident. He ascertained that Lena was killed instantly when her skull was smashed and only later did the car catch fire.

She had predicted this four days earlier, having observed that the lifeline in her hand was much like that in Florence's hand.

This was the first woman for six years who made an impression on me. (However, this after all, does not belong here.) Est had better drive a little more carefully.

Yours ever, E.

One of the many letters Dryden wrote to Hello from Paris on his own personally designed, headed notepaper. This letter in his extraordinary handwriting describes the accident with the Bugatti circa 1928.

DRYDEN · PARIS-NEUILLY · 30 RUE PERRONET

TÉLÉPHONE
MAILLOT 30-99

This was the other side to the times. Lena Amsel was a dancer with a lot of talent, and somehow the beauty of the design seems a little menacing after reading the letter.

Dryden's magazine advertising had very different requirements from his earlier poster art. He seems to have tended to the view that the magazine reader would in a sense have to fall in love with his design in order to fall in love with the object it advertised. Perhaps it is for this reason that his advertisements from this time are the only occasion in his career when Dryden becomes more geometric, in which objects are featured for themselves and human life, however unreal, disappears from the picture entirely. The discussion of the values of lettering and colours commenced by the Bauhaus was a subject of active discussion amongst all advertising artists. And instead of using standard forms of lettering that could be acquired, Dryden devised at least two whole alphabets of his own which he used with consistency.

The one he used most and which appears for the first time in the 1926 *Le Champion du Monde* Bugatti advert is perhaps more individual than the later Bauhaus sans serif as used in the blue Bugatti design. What Dryden was able to do by creating his own lettering, rather than using any standard typefaces, was to vary the proportions (not just size) according to the atmosphere of the subject in question. Therefore, the U of Bugatti is made wider than the U he used elsewhere, the two T's are joined together and the hook of the 6 in 1926 is able to hang on to the bottom rung of the E of Champion du Monde in the line above. The overall effect of this is to give the design a character unique to itself. There is a unity between image and lettering and the message is shared by both. In this way, Dryden accepted the current fashion and theory that a meaning could be shaped as much by the lettering as by the literal meaning of the words. Combining this concept with his previous interest in trademarks, his advertising work for Grütli Bière, Montre Zenith, Berliet, Botophon Haut-Parleur, Aladdin Crayons and Paris Matinal shows his reduction of message to its most minimal essence – economy of lettering, colour and image in one unity on the page.

It is a far cry from nightclub scenes of dancers and Berlin characters as depicted in his early poster art. It is almost unbelievable that in ten years his art can have changed so much. In the automotive design for Voisin he takes the silver wings of the vehicle's mascot which, set in silver, against the Voisin-blue background becomes a dramatic motif. It is a *tour de force*. He had created an advertisement for a car without showing anything but its trademark.

Dryden generally preferred to work with his own lettering – which had its built-in irregularities and character, rather than acquiring it wholesale. He used it again in the Cinzano advertisement of circa 1926, an item which, if not to everyone's taste, is certainly unforgettable. The centaur-like polo player is not a Dryden idea as such – other artists in Germany had used the anthropoid animal before, and Dryden had used a similar idea himself, depicting a cigarette-smoking jockey assimilated into a horse's body to advertise Manoli Cigarettes in 1911. But the re-working of the idea for Cinzano perhaps to indicate the perceived spiritual effects of the drink is almost surreal. It has elegance but it also has sexuality. At the time there was also a fashion for things African, a zebra was regarded as an outlandish creature. A *Vogue* cover from January 1926 also depicts a lady on a bucking zebra. In the bottom right-hand corner of Dryden's Cinzano advertisement Dryden's 'd' monogram itself peers somewhat eerily with its distinctive trademark of a disembodied staring eye. The advertisement may not have increased the sales of Cinzano but it certainly created a small piece of advertising history by its outlandish unforgettability.

In his advertisements for Blaupunkt – Waldorf Astoria the idea was to create a cigarette aimed at women. The *blau-punkt*, or blue dot, is used here as a trademark long before it was acquired by the makers of electronics and radio equipment, and it is possible that Dryden was the original creator of this mark. In the series he executed, which was published during 1928 in *Die Dame*, he effectively creates a composite portrait of the Blaupunkt woman. He creates quality for the brand with a mock authentic crest of coronet, oak leaves and gothic letters to symbolize the Waldorf Astoria, and the blue dots appear as a stylized form of smoke across the white gouache background. With only black and white body-colour for the main image the blue dots stand out unmistakably just as today this simple and yet perfect trademark is recognized everywhere.

Elsewhere in the series Dryden uses one of his favourite metamorphoses, that of the elegant lady who sprouts angel wings. As if the act of shopping is an indulgence of the Greek gods, the lady-in-waiting stands ready holding her mistress's wings, which will fly her, like Aphrodite, to her goal of the department store while, by her feet, instead of cupids, are her fluffy pedigree dogs.

Looking back on Dryden's advertising, we may see that it belongs, like his cover designs, to a period of advertising art when photography had not yet taken over; when magazines themselves were a more powerful medium, and the advertiser had concepts of design he wished his own products to aspire to. It was as if advertiser and artist were at times joined in a collaboration that still exudes the thrill of a creative adventure, not a purely money-making, sales-boosting tool. As art critic William Packer has said, 'there can be no practice where there is no work to be had' and when after the war advertisers turned almost exclusively to photography to serve their purposes, the skills of commercial artists like Dryden were no longer required. What we may see from Dryden's work is that knowledge of printing requirements and advertisers' needs, awareness of significant art movements, a strong basis of draughtsmanship and supreme imagination could combine to create a great advertisement.

Today they also show us something else, for through advertisements we can see expressions of the real tastes and desires of a generation. Indeed, perhaps in a hundred years when people wish to look back and see how people lived and worked, what entertained or interested them, the advertisement may tell us more than the rather isolated and pained art of the abstract painter.

Première pensée **sketch in pastel of a front cover idea for *Die Dame* circa 1927.**

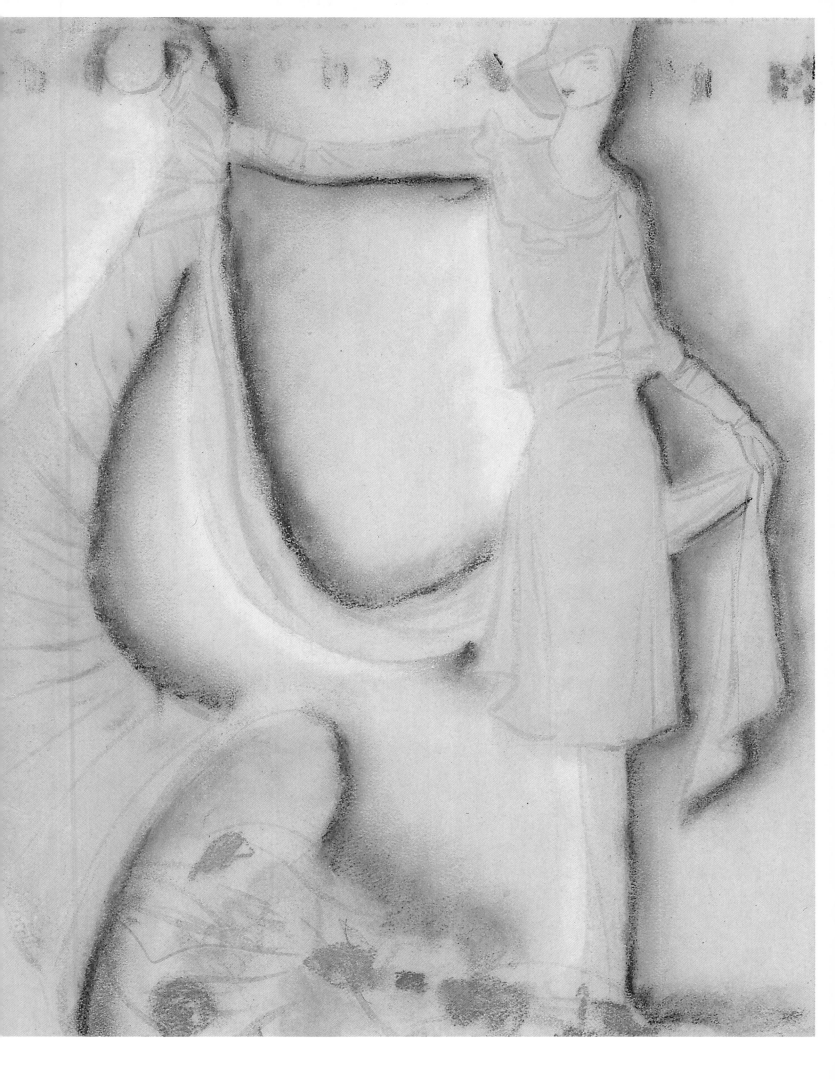

Front cover idea in wash and
watercolour on a cosmetic theme.

Opposite
Finished *Die Dame* front cover in pencil
and wash as it appeared in October
1929.

Première pensée in watercolour showing how Dryden developed his original idea for the *Die Dame* cover below, November 1928.

HEFT 3   ERSTES NOVEMBERHEFT   PREIS 1.50 MK.

Die Dame

*

VERLAG ULLSTEIN BERLIN

ZEICHNUNG VON DRYDEN

HEFT 3 · ERSTES NOVEMBERHEFT 1928 · PREIS 1,50 M

DIE ★ DAME ★

VERLAG
ULLSTEIN
BERLIN

AUTO ★ HEFT

Opposite

Die Dame front cover in gouache and pencil, November 1928. The yellow background became silver in the published version.

Die Dame front cover in gouache, watercolour and pencil, March 1930.

HEFT 17 ZWEITES MAIHEFT 1927

PREIS 1.50 MARK

DIE DAME

dryden

VERLAG
ULLSTEIN
BERLIN

Die Dame

1. Frühjahrsmodenheft

VERLAG ULLSTEIN, BERLIN

ZEICHNUNG VON DRYDEN

Die Dame illustration in gouache and pencil to accompany an article circa 1928.

Previous pages
Die Dame front cover, March 1927. The original does not exist and this is taken from the printed page.

Die Dame front cover in watercolour and pencil, undated.

Following pages
Unfinished advertisement for paint manufacturer I. G. Farben in pastel and gouache, 1928. The drawing was possibly executed in the paints that were being advertised.

Front cover design for *Die Dame* in gouache and pencil circa 1928.

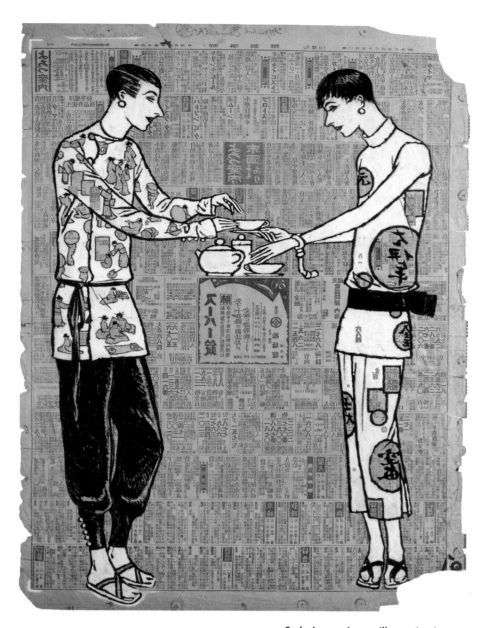

Style Japonais – an illustration in
gouache on a Japanese newspaper –
as it appeared in *Die Dame* 1927.

Opposite
Die Dame illustration of a flounce
dress in gouache and pencil circa 1928.

Die Dame front cover in gouache and
pencil on paper, October 1929.

Opposite
Finished artwork almost certainly for a
Die Dame cover in pencil and
watercolour on paper circa spring
1928.

Advertisement for Wolsey Swimwear in watercolour and pencil on tracing paper circa 1928.

Die Dame front cover in gouache and watercolour on paper, spring 1928.

Above
Illustration from *Die Dame* in watercolour and pencil, February 1930. The original measured 37x30cm but was finally printed in black and white hardly larger than a postage stamp.

Autumnal portrait in watercolour and pencil on paper from *Die Dame* circa 1930.

Opposite
Illustration from *TW Review* in gouache and pencil on paper, winter 1928.

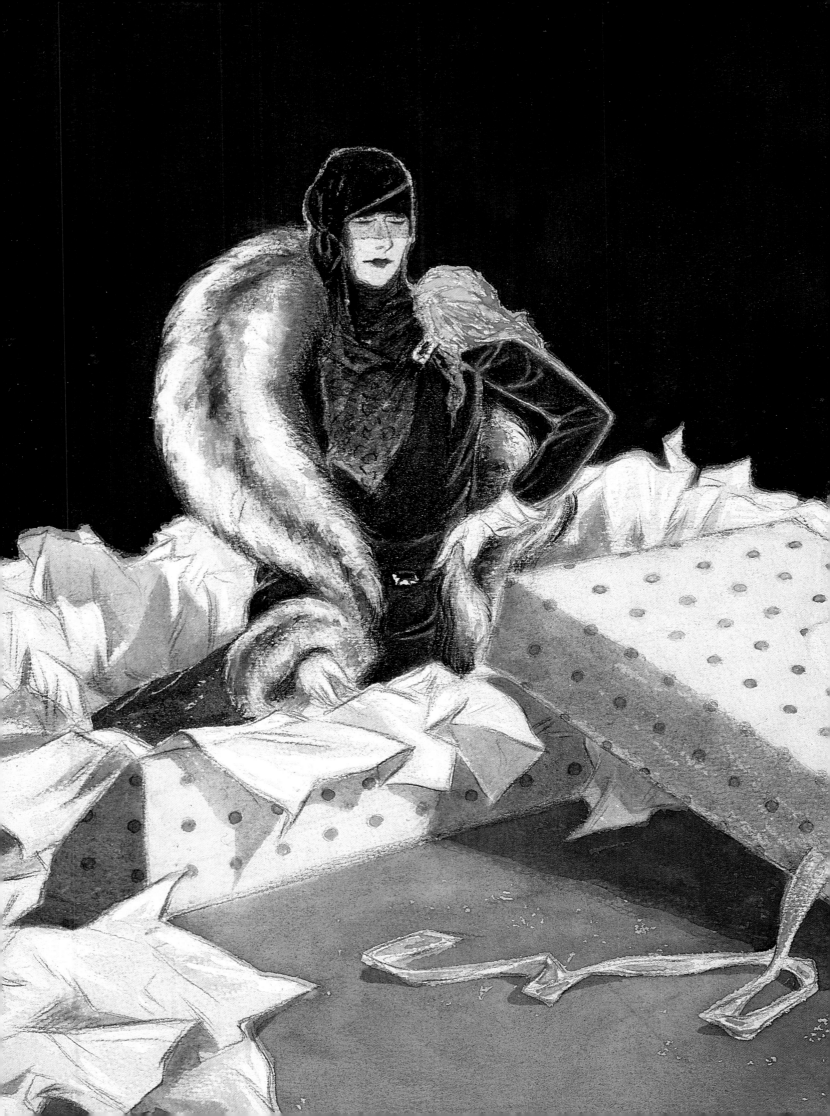

Opposite

Full-page illustration from *Die Dame*
entitled 'Beauty Competition for Cars'
in gouache and pencil, 1928. The scene
is the Bois de Boulogne in Paris and in
his mingling of civilian and military
dress Dyden has captured the lurking
menace behind the summer beauty.

Illustration for *Die Dame* in gouache,
pencil and watercolour on paper circa
1930.

Illustration for *Die Dame* in gouache,
pencil and watercolour on paper circa
1930.

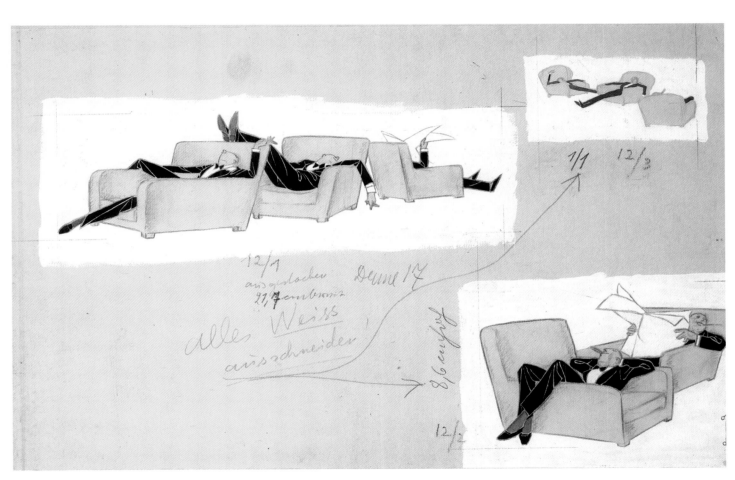

Illustration for an article in *Die Dame*
in gouache, ink and pencil on paper,
showing instructions to the printer,
circa 1928.

Illustration for *Die Dame* in pencil and watercolour on paper circa 1927, showing a further stage in the development of the Dryden monogram; the lower-case 'd' with eye motif will soon be detached from the rest of his name and become his inimitable trademark.

canadian
club ★ whisky

Box-top design in watercolour and
silver paint on card circa 1928.

JANE REGNY

Advertisement design for Jane Regny in gouache and pencil on paper as it appeared in French *Vogue*, June 1928. The car in the foreground is a Hispano-Suiza.

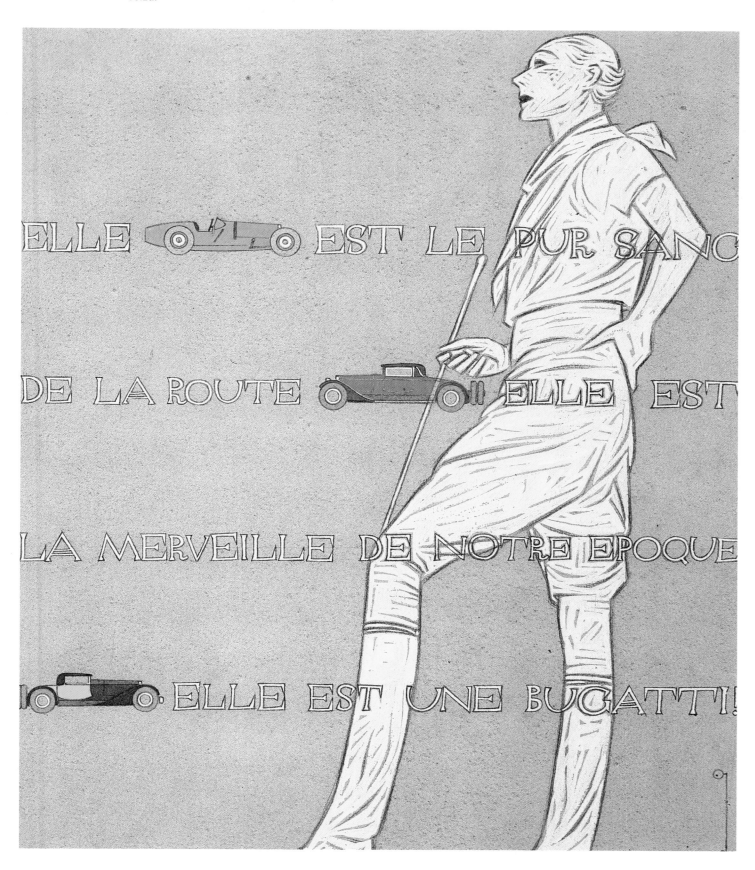

Advertisement design for Bugatti in gouache and watercolour on parchment-coloured paper circa 1928.

Advertisement portraying a lady, very
much resembling Hello, cutting the
fashions of the field, in watercolour
and pencil on paper, 1926.

Advertisement design for unknown
subject in gouache, watercolour and
pencil on paper circa 1928.

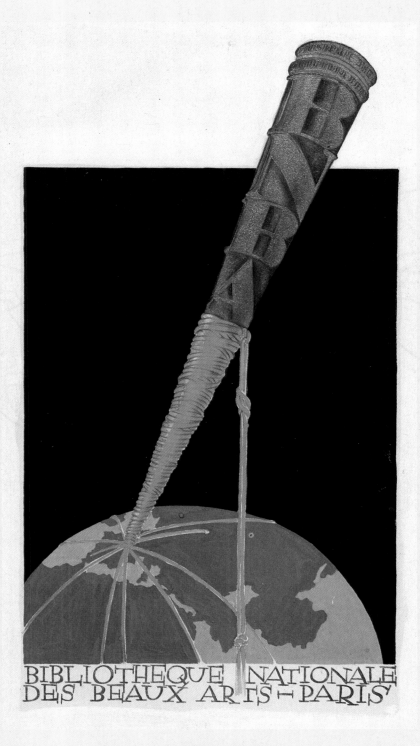

Advertisement design in gouache and
gold watercolour on paper for the
Bibliothèque Nationale des Beaux Arts,
Paris circa 1928.

Opposite
**Advertisement design for Zeus pencils
in gouache and pencil circa 1926.**

Advertisement design for Bugatti in
watercolour on paper, 1926.

Opposite
**Advertisement design for Bugatti in
gouache on card circa 1927.**

british
petrol

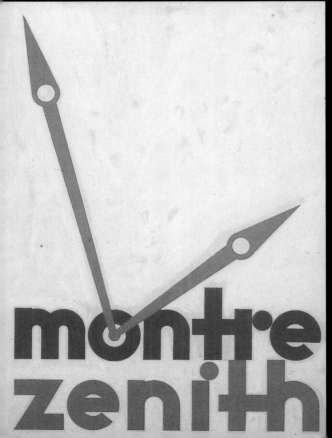

**Advertisement design for Berliet
Automobiles in watercolour and
gouache on paper circa 1927.**

**Advertisement design for Grütli Beer in
watercolour on paper circa 1927.**

**Advertisement design for Zenith Clocks
in watercolour and gouache on paper
circa 1927.**

Opposite
**Advertisement design for British Petrol
in watercolour on card circa 1927.**

**Advertisment design for Voisin
automobiles originally published in
Gebrauchsgraphik, in gouache and
silver paint on paper, 1929.**

Opposite
**Stone lithographic poster for the Paris
newspaper *Paris Matinal*, 1927.**

paris matinal

dryden

des imprimeries JOSÉ H CHARLES...

Second version of advertisement for
Cinzano with Max Beerbohm-style
caricature, in gouache on paper circa
1928.

Example of the centaur idea used by
Dryden at least fifteen years earlier to
advertise Manoli Cigarettes in
Elegante Welt.

Opposite
**Advertisement design for Cinzano in
gouache on card circa 1928.**

Advertisement designs for Blaupunkt
Waldorf-Astoria Cigarettes and
published in *Die Dame*, 1928.

Sei ein Geschenk noch so bescheiden, darf es
nicht minder achtsame und liebevolle Wahl
verraten. Schenkt eine Dame Zigaretten,
wird sie daher nur eine Marke wählen,
deren Name Begriff wurde für »Zigarette«.

BLAUPUNKT

Jene Frauen, welche am Geschehen der Zeit teilnehmen, jener Typ, der mit „Frau von heute" bezeichnet wird, ist es, der uns fesselt. Frauen, welche urteilsfähig sind, Qualitätsgefühl haben und ihr Heim kultivieren. Frauen, die ihrer Gastgeberpflicht bewußt, auch scheinbar Nebensächlichem Bedeutung beimessen und Zigaretten ebenso achtsam bereitstellen, wie etwa Weine und Liköre.

B L W A A L A U P D U O R F N A K T

DRESS DESIGN

Photograph of Ernst Dryden shortly after his arrival in New York in 1934.

O N T H E E V E of his departure for America, on 20 November 1933, Dryden had written his will. It was perhaps with deep foreboding for the future that he did this. 'I am an old man,' he wrote to Hello a few months later. 'Hello doesn't realize this.'

He did not know if this latest move was going to be a success. All he did know was that the situation in Europe would get worse. Presumably he also knew that he was going to be fighting against illness, for he had been diagnosed as having Graves' disease – a condition which affected the heart. And yet, on 22 February 1934, only three months later, writing from The Ambassador Hotel, Park Avenue, New York, he was able to say to Hello: 'I am working hard. The difficulties are great, my sensitivity is no small thing and it's extremely hard for me – but I have come here with the same programme as I did when I went to Paris, and I believe I shall carry it through, in spite of anything that stands in my way.'

He didn't have long to wait. On 3 March he wrote, 'I am waiting for the launch of my collection and then we shall see. I have done some very good work (so long as my boss does not spoil it with her own creations!)' By 16 March, less than two weeks later, he is brimming with excitement as if he has already made it: 'The start was so successful that people are scrambling for me now. I don't know who the winner will be. It is like a lottery!'

America was fabled as a land of opportunity, but by any standards this was a speedy start. Soon he was designing for Saks Fifth Avenue, Macy's, Marshall Field & Co and Germaine Monteil. His output was as prolific as ever, and his consumption of paper enormous. He used to sketch on the back of Germaine Monteil order forms, and he got through pad after pad.

His style had changed with the move to America. Never one to favour an overworked style, his lines had become ever freer and, if possible, more assured. The composite American lady he designed for was different from the European. She was taller, fairer, thinner. She was open to new ideas. She was not trapped in old world culture. It allowed Dryden the freedom to be inventive again in new and stimulating ways.

There were always those Europeans who could not adjust to America, and others whose curiosity was given a new lease of life, as if Europe had dulled their senses. On 16 March he wrote to Hello again: 'The school here I am going through is invaluable, I have learned thousands of things in four months here! . . . Paul [Paul Budischowsky, Hello's third husband, who was a belt manufacturer] will be thrilled when he sees the kind of *drills* there are around!'

Inevitably, we also see how, through those troubled times, the worries of Europe rise to the surface in each letter. Worries for Hello . . . what to do . . . where to go? . . . whether to stay . . . Through the miasma of unclear events, we see the crazy or not so crazy schemes of salvation which were considered. 3 March: 'Bali seems a great idea . . . though the people there don't need many clothes . . .'

We see how Hello features in his deepest plans and desires. 16 March: 'I am tremendously happy when I read Hello's report about peace. I see dear Papa [Paul Budischowsky] in a deck chair and Peter [the dog] digging the garden . . . Our future will be in peaceful work together, to share all the difficulties as well as the happiness. This alone can give our lives deep meaning which alone makes life worth living.'

It is as if to envisage a state of union and harmony through creative work is one of his highest ideals. It is something he and Hello had striven for, and which they

Previous page
New York evening-wear design with outsize fur cuffs in watercolour and pencil on paper circa 1934.

seemed to continue to work towards right up until the end of his life. But he did not indulge in these Utopian thoughts for too long. More commonly he exhorted Hello once again to work and to be defiant: 'We have a duty to defend our lives and not to go under,' he says, adding later, 'I always work best when there is shooting outside . . . '

He had made it. And yet even when the sweet scent of success was hardly fresh in the air he was saying: 'In spite of this success (it is the best collection I have ever made) I hardly think I shall stay here [New York]. I have already started other things.' And within a few months of this time, and with no time to lose, he was commencing his career in Hollywood.

At the base of Dryden's many interlocking talents was always his skill as a dress designer. His move to New York, when he had to return to basics, meant he had to use those skills again to the full. Although they had never really slumbered, not until New York were they to be his total livelihood. So it is worth considering for a moment what Dryden's roots as a dress designer actually were and what were the principles that motivated him in his designs.

A good analogy is afforded by another comparison with the work of Adolf Loos. What Adolf Loos had said about architecture, Ernst Dryden believed about fashion. 'Ornament is crime,' Loos had said, and just as in Loos's architecture functionality was the main arbiter of taste, so it was also with all Dryden's dress and menswear design.

With regard to the decisions about what to wear and on what occasion, Dryden was a 'classicist', not an innovator. Novelty for novelty's sake alone was unlikely to produce good design. An example he himself often gave was this: you can be wearing the most beautiful dress in the world, but if you are going out for a walk in the woods you are going to look ridiculous. Instead, fitness for purpose and appropriateness of colours, shades, textiles, cuts, should be, according to Dryden, the primary objectives of the fashion designer.

At the same time, when Loos mentioned the word function he did not mean that all his architecture should be reduced to functionalism – it just should be usable. Loos was merely contrasting himself with the historicism of the Vienna architecture of his period which was represented by all the neo-classic facades of the Ringstrasse, full of pomp and circumstance but with little content. As he writes in one of his essays, it was like those little Russian villages, consisting entirely of facades, that Catherine II's adviser Potemkin built to give the Tsarina the impression of populated towns as she rode through an undeveloped area. When Loos designed flat roofs it was because he believed that was the best way of designing a roof.

Like Loos, Dryden was fascinated by materials. Perhaps materials were one of the prime inspirations he worked from as a dress designer. Many of his drawings still had swatches attached. They included satins, linens, velvets, silks, chiffons, taffetas. And in each drawing the very nature of that material is brought out. A tweed on a Dryden drawing really looks like a tweed; you can almost feel its texture. The use of the material was inspired by the various activities of the civilized person in a social context. The main activities were town life in one of the great capitals – Vienna, Paris, London – and relaxation in the country.
The full range of activities says more today about the market for which he was designing than anything else, and inevitably whole areas such as evening wraps or cocktail dresses have decreased in importance over the years. A look through

PRINCIPLES
OF
DRESS
DESIGN

Dryden's folders with his bold headings daubed across the front gives an indication of the range of wear he designed for:

Cocktail	*Blouses, Skirts,*	*Dressy Suits*
Beach Wear	*Dresses*	*Street Dresses*
Afternoon Cocktail	*Coats*	*Evening Wraps*
Evening Dresses	*Sports Dresses*	*Complets*

To be well dressed was to be able to wear the right things on the right occasion. For a woman this was always going to be more agonizing than for a man, and Dryden's working folder titles indicate some of the options she had.

Just as no two occasions are ever the same, so in over two thousand of Dryden's dress designs, there is never a standard face. Instead he seems to have needed to visualize, albeit with the minimum of detail, an actual pose for his imagined model – whether it is leaning, resting a hand, holding a bag or carrying a staff for a country walk.

Some of the drawings were probably intended to be shown in the shop window, as indeed they were at Hello's shop on the Graben, so that a passer-by spotting a beautiful hand-drawn design in the window and a made-up version of the garment next to it would walk in and demand something similar.

Smartness, for Dryden, was not a dictate issued from a fashion house. Having discovered an appropriateness of dress to purpose, the customer in the shop or boutique then had another important choice to make with the aid of his own tailor or dressmaker. What suits me? What suits the person for whom the design was made? A scribbled note on the back of one design for an evening dress gives an indication of the relationship between dressmaker and client. It reads: 'Can't I have another colour. I look like the devil in pink!' It was not sufficient to have the best materials, the best design and then expect a woman or man to look perfect – it had to suit.

What this meant is that Dryden, while a man of fashion, did not follow each of its dictates. He could be dictatorial himself, but only in principles of design – where to position a pocket or how to cut a sleeve – not in imposing taste. At best, taste was going to be a harmony of materials to purpose and this could only be worked out individually.

The principle of looking well dressed was a fascinating topic. It had occupied Loos in several of his essays from his book *Ins Leere Gesprochen* (Falling on deaf ears). He begins his essay on 'Men's Fashion', originally published in *Neue Freie Presse* in 1898, as follows: 'To be well dressed – who does not want to be well dressed?'

Born in 1870, Loos was 17 years Dryden's senior, and it was Dryden who saw a world of fashion emerge that began to take on the shape that Loos had predicted. Loos had mentioned in another article on *Ladies Fashion* also published in *Neue Freie Presse* in 1898, the emancipating nature of women's fashion. By the time Dryden was designing it had all come true – the woman was already emancipated; she was freer to work, and had become more economically independent.

If we look directly at Dryden's drawings again we can see that many of his creations incorporate these social facts within their design; in particular the lady's two-piece suit – the best example of tidy town wear – expresses this independence perfectly. It is a favourite garment; one that treats a lady seriously. Its beauty is its simplicity and quality of cut and texture, its ability to give the woman respect in her town environment. One thing it doesn't do is breathe sexuality. It is remarkably asexual.

Loos had foreseen this, predicting in mock psycho-analytical manner that the lady would no longer need protection by the 'big strong man' stereotype. She did not any longer need to exploit her sensuality in dress with 'silk, flowers and ribbons, feathers and paints'. Fashion was no longer purely theatrical.

But what type of woman was Dryden working for? By now she was neither as young and frivolous as the girlish *ingénues* idealized by writers and artists immediately after the First World War, nor as sexually daring or decadent as the Germanic vamp figure of some of the early posters. She was now a fully-fledged individual, a member of society. She was political rather than weak. She was dressed for taking the side of her man if she chose – not for coming out like some wondrous feathered creature to be displayed to guests. This type of woman commanded respect because she dominated the fashion business. Its greatest proponent was a woman – Chanel herself. Without overt sexuality the woman has found a new role. So Dryden shows her wearing clothes that are serious, as befits the role of a woman who takes herself seriously.

Interior view of the advertising and publicity department of Simpson's of Piccadilly. Staff are working here from Dryden designs flown in from Paris circa 1933.

One of Dryden's greatest interests in the dress design field for women was his study of sportswear. It is one of the great chics of fashion, still valid today, that the movement in tastes in clothes usually moves from the sportswear area into everyday. Sportswear usually in time becomes formal wear. The best male example of this is the tailcoat, which comes from the riding habit. For the female it was the tweeds, jerseys, woollen jumpers that Dryden wanted to bring indoors or allow the woman to use as formal wear.

It was partly the increasing sophistication of transport systems within town life which led to these changes. It was more practical to have layers of clothing that could be easily removed and easily put back on. Temperatures from warm salons to cold streets could vary enormously, and with people coming and going so much it was inconvenient to be so formally clad that these adjustments to dress were a complication. Clothes developed for sport always had a harmony of style and purpose.

Another of Dryden's favourite garments is the coat – in camel, Burberry or check. It always looked relaxed and tidy, easy to unbutton or to remove. Underneath, the tweeds and woollens could match perfectly. An added touch was the scarf, which was the link between indoor and outdoor, a little temperature valve of its own that could be adjusted to please. Dryden particularly liked polka dots on a coloured background, because they were fun and added a spark of brightness to outdoor colours.

Dryden created Hello after his own image unrestricted by the specific house style of any other company. Sportswear, outdoor, walking wear was undoubtedly the shop's strong point. Even the Hello lettering Dryden devised across a number of the designs looks as if it was created with a piece of woollen thread. With the Austrian climate of lakes and mountains, scarves and coats predominate. He makes a feature out of long outside lapels and huge buttons on a camel coat. The belt should never be done up exactly but knotted informally. It should be possible to raise the lapels to cover the neck to shelter from icy winds. It must look good from the back too – with baggy shoulders and arms juxtaposed with the natural pleated fall of the material. Pockets are another feature. For the country, lots of pockets. They are useful. Some rounded at the base, others squared. Not hidden away but made as a feature.

Back indoors again, the lady should be able to adjust her dress to suit her; that is to say the garment should be able to be worn as elegantly buttoned or unbuttoned, it should be able to show her blouse or not, as preferred. Belts could be fun too. They were a continually varied and adaptable feature, at one and the same time linking and separating top and bottom halves. Hidden when clothes are buttoned, revealed at a more casual moment.

Being an Austrian shop, Hello was in the forefront of what is today a big industry – ski wear. Ski wear has always been a favourite of designers, as it is an opportunity to get involved with some traditional patterns and embroideries which would be impractical elsewhere. Dryden took a Tyrolean or mountain people's motif and created a stylish braided top for the lady. The gloves had an embroidered pine cluster motif, the thick socks providing a splash of colour at the base of long plain pants. A metal ring tag (perhaps for attaching the gloves later) was made of silver with an 'H' motif on its leather thong. Elsewhere the men looked best in Norwegian knitted sweaters with snowflake patterns.

In total contrast, Dryden also created some swimwear which is truly astonishing in its modernity. Now that the bikini is no longer so dominant, Dryden's designs with cross-over patterns and flesh-revealing angles look stunning in their freedom and make the point that while the bikini has gone out of fashion today, his designs would still be in.

But essentially there is one big difference that separates Dryden's Viennese work from his creations in New York. All Dryden's designs for Hello belong to the age of the personal dressmaker. Each of Hello's customers chose and acquired something unique for herself. Every customer was different, and no two dresses were the same. In New York Dryden's customers were no longer individuals but the big stores. He had become a designer for the ever expanding ready-to-wear market, in the biggest and most competitive market in the world.

New York

In America in 1934 the fashionable lady was quite happy to buy from the ready-to-wear market. Unlike her European sister, the American woman did not need to know that her garment was unique in order to have confidence in her own style. In this sense the American lady was more practical, she had moved with the times, and Dryden would have undoubtedly approved of this. Indeed, he seems to have been inspired by the thought that his designs would reach a far wider audience than ever before.

Stores like Saks or Macy's cultivated their female buyers in a different way to the personal dressmaker. Even in the way in which a dress would be tried on was a different type of experience. The store pandered to the woman's wish to be seen, rather than her wish for privacy. To carry a label from Saks was as good as from a personal designer, as Saks was better known. Furthermore, a big store like Saks could react to changes and fads more quickly. A good example of this is the way Dryden himself was later to adapt designs from the films he was working on for retail sale. Women who saw Jane Wyatt in her costumes from *Lost Horizon* (1937) or Grace Moore in *The King Steps Out* (1937) wanted the same, and the stores could satisfy that demand on a big scale. The stores realized the power of the films to influence taste, and catered to it. One can imagine the European lady sticking her nose in the air at the thought of wearing imitations of film costumes – but in America this was a bestseller.

So, with his move to New York, Dryden had entered an entirely new market, and part of the reason for his immediate success must have been his prompt recognition of this. His style changed and he designed for the new market with the utmost vigour. Outdoor designs, typical of Europe, were discarded. The European love of looking outdoors while being indoors was never a particularly American trait anyway. Instead, the lady who was spending on a dress wanted to look like a million dollars, and Dryden appears to have searched for and found forms which would achieve this effect without garishness, without excess decoration and at a reasonable cost.

He seems to have found part of the inspiration for this in the styles of classical Greece and Rome. It was as if America, through Dryden's eyes, was the new Rome. It was a country of power, whose people were proud, brave and rich. He could be more dramatic than he could have been in Europe. Perhaps this is why some of Dryden's dress designs from New York are almost indistinguishable from his later Hollywood film costume designs, and also why a lot of his Hollywood material was later adapted for retail sale.

What he drew on from classical forms was the ability for clothes to be apparently sylph-like and insubstantial to a degree that the European lady was not yet ready for. The waist could be dramatically high; but not like the so-called Empire-line of 1912, holding up heavy materials. *Décolleté* or off-the-shoulder gowns could be light, like his later design for Madeleine Carroll as Queen of Ruritania in *The Prisoner of Zenda*. The ancient Greeks and Romans were true examples for him, for their ideas of dress conformed to simple rules. A material could be used, toga-like, to bring out aspects of freedom of movement. A clasp could hold the bodice, fake white laurel leaves form the straps, a cluster of beads serve as a brooch – but no other ornament. One design is a white sheath almost without seams, knotted nonchalantly at the top with a big blue bow, as if to undo the bow would cause the whole item to collapse to the floor.

When Dryden moved to Hollywood, after less than a year in New York, he never gave up designing for the mass market. But in becoming a costumier he did return to the last bastion of perfectionism and personal attention. Who could embody this demand better than the star for whom he was soon to be personal costumier – Marlene Dietrich – the most meticulously dressed star of them all!

Pencil sketches on the back of
Germaine Monteil New York order
paper, 1934.

Three designs for *Hello*.

Clockwise
Check two-piece suit in pencil and watercolour on paper, 1934.

Tweed skirt and suede jacket in pencil and watercolour on paper, 1934.

Fur coat with high collar and matching skirt in pencil and watercolour on paper, 1934.

Two-piece day suit with long jacket based on painter's overalls in pencil and watercolour, 1933.

Loden jacket and complet for town and country in pencil and watercolour, 1933.

Lady's mackintosh with polka-dot scarf
in pencil and watercolour on paper,
1932-3.

Following pages
Two early ski-wear designs featuring
traditional Austrian embroidered
motifs in pencil and watercolour, 1932.

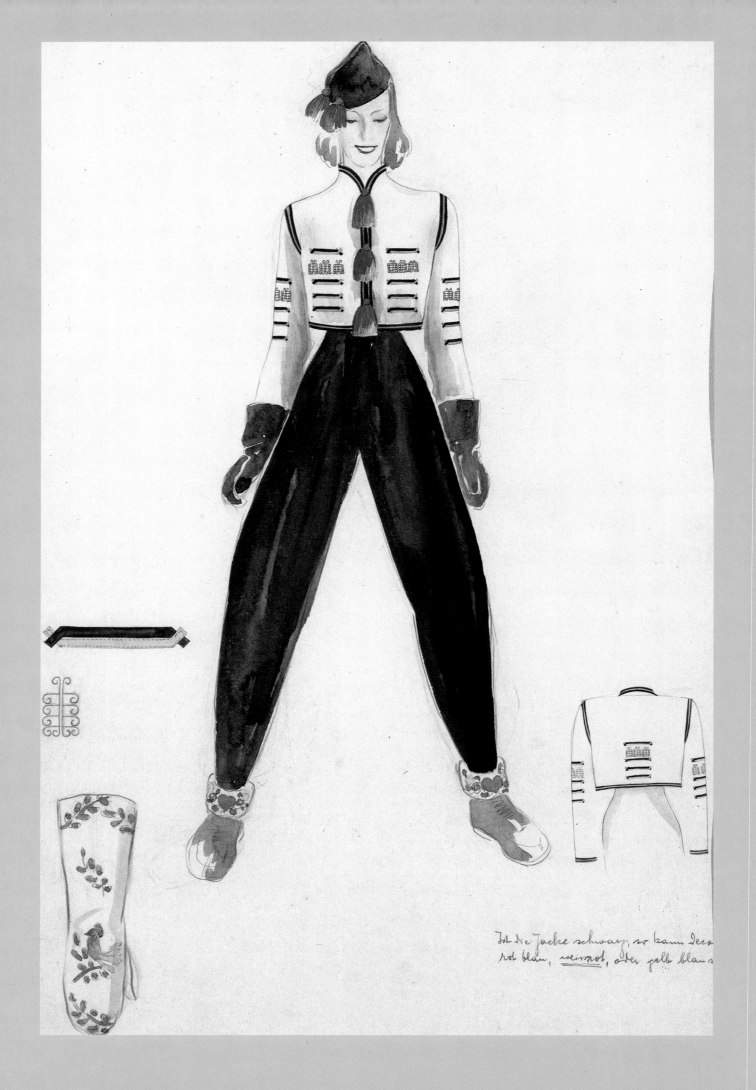

Three examples of swimwear in pencil
and watercolour on paper circa 1934.

Top **Smoky-pink sheath evening dress in pencil and watercolour on paper, 1934.**

Bottom **Evening dress in grey for Saks Fifth Avenue in pencil and watercolour on paper, 1934.**

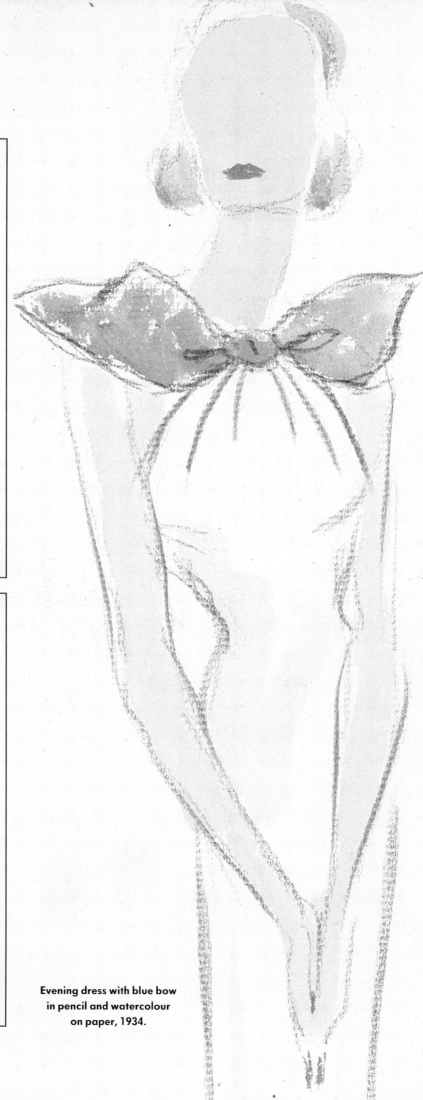

Evening dress with blue bow in pencil and watercolour on paper, 1934.

Design for evening dress with velvet
fabric sample attached, labelled The
Herald Silk Shop, New York, in pencil,
ink and watercolour on paper.

Opposite
Summer lightweight evening dress
nipped in at the waist in pencil and
gouache on card, 1934.

**The Garden of Allah Hotel, 8152
Sunset Boulevard as it looked in 1935
when Dryden was living there.**

Previous pages
**'That dress', the chiffon dress for
Marlene Dietrich in *The Garden of
Allah* (1936) in pencil and light wash,
and a photographic still of Dietrich
wearing the dress on set.**

*P*ERHAPS one particular costume in a single film sums up Dryden's
Hollywood achievement better than anything else – Marlene Deitrich's
white chiffon dress in the film *The Garden of Allah* (1936), with its
swirling chic veils designed to pick up the cool desert breezes.

The plot of the film concerns a virginal, solitude-seeking religious convert –
played by Dietrich – who encounters an attractive and debonair escaped
trappist monk – Charles Boyer – just fled from his desert enclave. Perhaps
unexpectedly, the Dietrich character, Domini Einfelden, rather than encouraging
him to return to worldly life eventually escorts him back to the monastery gates.

It was filmed near Yuma, on the borders of the Nevada desert which was
doubling as the Sahara, and the famous chiffon dress, partly at least, was
intended to show off the mechanical prowess of the wind machine, or Ritter, as it
was called after its inventor. 'That dress', as it became known, was in fact one of
the saving graces of a film which was beset with problems. Until recently, Dietrich
herself has said little about it, but in her autobiography she has written about the
film and its problems, and also, with some affection, about her costumier.

In spite of the films' many failings, it is impossible not to admire the incidental
by-product of it all – the heavenly fashion show in the desert, which was Dryden's
creation. It also records once again on film the wondrous beauty and attraction
of Dietrich herself.

But *The Garden of Allah* is significant in film history from another point of view
entirely – for it was one of the first ever films to be made in Technicolor. What
seems to have happened, in fact, was that in the search for a vehicle to test out
the new Technicolor process, David Selznick, the film's producer, obscured the
need to produce a marketable film. He was not alone. Knowing that colour was
the new and exciting aspect of the film which might make it a box-office success,
it seems that crew, directors and actors alike became over-absorbed with this at
the expense of real drama. The entanglements with the process itself, as well as
filming in the desert heat, became a drain on everyone's resources and energy. A
good example of the kind of problem they faced is recorded by Dietrich: when
cast and crew returned for final filming at the studio, they found that the desert
sands imported into the studio from the Indian Ocean rather than the Pacific were
now the wrong colour. These were problems which had never been encountered
before and which ultimately affected the film.

On the positive side there were many significant aspects to the film from the
point of view of the development of colour in film as a whole. Dietrich records
how with Dryden and Selznick she had decided that her costumes would use only
shades of colour that would occur in the desert. No one had ever had this luxury
before, and it seems to have gone to her head. What neither she nor anyone else
could have known then was that the race for colour would be a surprisingly
stop-start affair and that many great films – *Sunset Boulevard* for example, made
over fourteen years later – could and did succeed without this innovation.

One of the specific difficulties of the Technicolor process consisted of the fact
that the cameras had to be rented from the inventors, the Kalmuses; a further
problem being that the main wish of Natalie Kalmus, wife of the inventor, was to
show off the garish Technicolor dyes as much as possible. This fascinating and
historic conflict is actually recorded in one of over 1,900 file-boxes of Selznick's
memos currently housed at Texas University and it particularly records the clash
between the subtle aims of Dryden and Dietrich on the one hand, and the sheer
gaudiness of Kalmus on the other. That Dietrich and Dryden in fact won this battle

had huge implications for one film at any rate. Had they not succeeded, *Gone with the Wind*, produced by Selznick two years later, might have been a very different film to look at. And had Dryden lived perhaps he would have been costumier.

What remains of wonderful interest from *The Garden of Allah*, a piece of ephemera that was preserved with the rest of Dryden's surviving papers, is the actual colour-coding Dryden worked out to be picked up by Technicolor at the process stage. In other words, Dryden, trusting only himself, was setting the colour values by his trained eye. Mrs Kalmus's job was to match them. The final result, colour-wise, is impressive and atmospheric and Dietrich, speaking of the subtlety with which colour was created, still calls it in her autobiography 'the most beautiful colour film ever made'. Had its Russian-born director, Richard Boleslavski, not been ill (he was to die shortly after filming ceased), perhaps something more could have been made of it.

There were numerous parts for which designs were needed: Arabs, dancers, street urchins — a marvellous character of a Jewess who never seems to have been used — 'Hadj' the faithful Arab guide, foreign legion soldiers: all are imaginatively created with Dryden's famous lightness of touch. Not for Dryden the usual stiff or overworked orientalism. And yet, while the setting was meant to be exotic, it was only meant to be 'Hollywood exotic'. The characters were dressed for desert settings in order to show off how cool and veiled they could look against an oriental setting which never becomes more substantial than a backdrop.

In four weeks of shooting Dietrich alone had approximately thirty costume changes. Dryden, meticulous as he was, recorded each of these in miniature on a storyboard which he created for this purpose, listing the scenes, with date and brief description, sometimes with added swatch of suede or chiffon attached: 'De Trevignac dinner', 'Confession Sequence' and 'Wedding' were some of the scene headings. The same designs were made in large format too, and some, such as Dietrich's riding costume, showing her propensity for masculine garments, looked stunning. Just a selection of her costumes includes a lunch dress, white coat, wedding dress, travel suit, balcony dress, torch dress, dinner dress, confession dress, café dress and négligée. The fabrics for these included black satin, silver lamé, white chiffon, gunmetal and elephant satin, orchid, pink and blue-grey chiffons, natural coloured wools and leather.

The photograph of Dietrich and Dryden as they stand together in the off-set still against the backdrop of the palms — she in her jodhpurs and turban — is a touching record of the relationship between star and costumier. For, as Dietrich herself has said, she chose Dryden as her costumier. She would have known of his career as illustrator for *Die Dame*, of his early posters in Berlin and perhaps even of his association with the menswear tailors Knize. (When Knize opened a store in New York, she even used them herself!)

It had been artists like Dryden who had helped to create the Berlin idyll, and in their success they had been as famous as film stars themselves in the ferment of Austria and Germany. Indeed the so-called look that is Dietrich, the vanity or haughtiness of the *femme fatale*, was a pose that Dryden might well be said to have created himself many times for the women who bedecked the pages of *Die Dame*. The essence of chic which Dietrich recreated on film was its celluloid equivalent. The model for all these women had been actual life in Berlin — something they both knew well.

Dryden's colour-coding palette for application in the Technicolor process which he sketched on The Garden of Allah Hotel's headed notepaper while staying there in 1935 during filming of *The Garden of Allah* (1936).

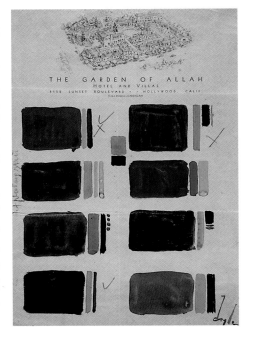

A fleeting portrait of Marlene Dietrich and costume design for a gunmetal satin negligée for *The Garden of Allah* (1936) in pencil and watercolour on paper.

Whatever their association was beyond the roles of star and film costumier it is impossible to say – that Dietrich fascinated Dryden as much as she fascinated anyone may be seen by the way he drew her. He seems unable to design for her without attempting to capture something more of her than the mere design of costume would have required. He was clearly captivated and the designs that remain are portraits in themselves – perhaps the only ones that exist of Dietrich on paper rather than film. Again and again, he seems fascinated by her eyes or, more specifically, those high eyebrows which were her trademark. Dryden, the great designer and originator of real trademarks, seemed to see all the stars – these larger than life personalities – through their own trademarks. For Dietrich this was without question her eyes, the softness behind elongated eyelashes and the art deco of her eyebrows.

Although Dryden rarely if ever painted portraits in the conventional sense, it is interesting to note that, as Dietrich's costumier, he would have been in a position to depict her over more sittings than most portrait painters would have been granted. If Dryden's picture of her appears fleeting, that is in the nature of costume art. We appear to glimpse her, veiled but unmistakable, through the more mundane process of the creation of her costume.

On other subjects too Dryden, unlike many costumiers, almost always depicts the exact character of the actor or actress within his drawings (if casting had already taken place), as if he needed to capture this essence to create the relationship between star and costume. Working also on *The Garden of Allah* in the part of a dancer was the Austrian actress Tilly Losch. It is intriguing to wonder how she fitted into this German-speaking triangle. In Europe she had been a Max Reinhardt protégée, starring in *The Miracle*, as well as some of Bertholt Brecht's dramas. Perhaps she felt that Dryden devoted too much time and attention to Dietrich, because she alone records in her personal diary some unkind words for Dryden. If we are to believe her own version of events, she approved neither of Dryden's designs nor of his personality. Her record at some time in 1935 was as follows: 'Tried to get Oliver Messel as my costumier. But another Austrian has sketched for me – Mr E. Dryden – and they are incredibly banal. I tried to be considerate to him (he is frightfully arrogant and stupid and talks too much) but I cannot risk anything on my first picture.'

In fact, it sounds as if not all the arrogance was on Dryden's side. Tilly Losch goes on to say within the same section, even before her film debut, that all she wanted was to find a rich man and get married. It was a plan she soon put into practice, becoming perhaps more famous as the wife of the English eccentric Edward James than she would have been as a film star. In spite of this, the designs Dryden did for her are some of his best, full of movement and colour, the only time Dryden appears to venture in the direction of Leon Bakst or the Ballet Russe style of design.

Dryden's career in Hollywood is bound up with the general notion of Hollywood exiles or what film critic John Russell Taylor has called *Strangers in Paradise*. Dryden's personal story is part of this theme – the exile, in his case voluntary, having to start a career in a new country, in a new language and again in his case in a new medium too. Even by the time Dryden arrived, the burial ground containing the extinguished careers of others who had passed along this way was filling up. A measure of Dryden's achievement is that none of these factors proved a hindrance to him but, as on previous occasions, adversity seemed a spiritual resource.

An important distinction should be made between his road to Hollywood and that of some who had preceded him. Ten years earlier the influx of Europeans was economically led. The US studios had seen a threat from the government-sponsored German film industry and bought up as much of the talent as possible. A few years later it was motivated by charity when the movie houses created, at the instigation of the US government, a small number of blank contracts to enable writers and artists under threat from the Nazis to get out of Europe. Dryden was one of a small band of personalities who had taken an independent decision for his own reasons and arrived alone, taking the risk upon himself. Dietrich's case was similar, and so was that of the young Billy Wilder. When it came to their moral standpoint they shared the same philosophical high ground. They knew why they were in Hollywood. It was a brave attempt for sensitive and artistic people to survive and succeed in a free country in the world's most competitive industry.

It is this sense of triumph – one he would not have mentioned to friends – which Dryden reveals in writing to Hello. On 28 March 1935, on headed notepaper from The Garden of Allah Hotel, 8152 Sunset Boulevard, he wrote:

Once again Dryden has made his way into a foreign country overnight and made an impact too. If nothing goes seriously wrong – it was a brilliant and unique start even for Hollywood – my career will be so to speak established. It means much, a great deal indeed, because nowhere in the world are things more difficult. Over here you can't be bluffing . . .

And Dryden was not a man to bluff . . . Back in Vienna those letters were read with excitement and hope. Did Hello think she would ever join him in America? It does not really seem so. But leave Austria? Yes. That was imperative. Dryden had repeated this advice to her many times but in a less decisive manner with respect to her than he had been with himself. At one time he had recommended her to set up in Prague; at others, while acknowledging the 'shooting in the street', he still implored her to redouble her efforts, to go to Berlitz and learn English. He was always saying this to her, 'You must learn English!'

Dryden's route to Hollywood reflected above all his continued belief in himself. 'Dryden' was going to succeed. Arriving in 1934 with his destiny in his pocket, he had no need to be too humble. He had arrived with sufficient means, just as he had done when he moved from Vienna to Paris. Who knows, perhaps his stake in Hello's business in Vienna was a kind of insurance policy, meaning that if, unexpectedly, Europe should settle down and Hollywood turn bad, he could return; in other words, that he had not burnt all his boats in Europe. But the reality was that he cannot have expected to return. He saw the European situation far too clearly for that.

Having sufficient money, Dryden started work from The Garden of Allah Hotel. From here he probably completed work on *Remember Last Night?* and *Lost Horizon* and soon *The Garden of Allah*, the film of the same name. In such a short time in Hollywood he worked on a high proportion of interesting films.

The Garden of Allah Hotel and Apartments, now razed to the ground, was the creation of Nazimova, the Russian star of the 1920s silents, mentor to Rudolph Valentino's wife Natacha Rambova. It was a famous meeting ground for various refugees. Originally the hotel was Nazimova's splendid home, and after becoming the centre of Hollywood society it was then turned into a hotel, changing its name from The Garden of Alla to The Garden of Allah at about this

Marguerite Churchill modelling a Dryden gown for retail based on the original creation for *The Lady of Athens* (1937).

time. By staying there, Dryden had his finger on the pulse of a certain part of Hollywood society into which he would have been immediately accepted as a leading member. Like Dietrich they would all have known of his past achievements. At forty-eight he had plenty left in him, it seemed, both in years and temperament, unlike Heinrich Mann, the author of *The Blue Angel*, by now almost seventy and unable to write another screenplay. As ever, Dryden's progress was swift. By late 1936 he was able to buy a house at 459 South Bentley Avenue, west of Bel Air and on the south side of Sunset Boulevard.

Nothing sums up his social environment better than the photograph taken on his lawn in the summer of 1937. The most elegant man at the front right is Ernst Dryden, behind left a young Billy Wilder, at the back Mr and Mrs Peter Lorre, on the ground next to him in glasses Karl Vollmöller, author of *The Miracle*, the famous play which once starred Lady Diana Cooper and included the dancing of Tilly Losch, produced by Max Reinhardt. At other times, at other parties, there was Ernst Lubitsch, Heinrich and Thomas Mann, Arnold Schoenberg, John Brahm, Dolly Haas.

Oscar-winning costumier Dorothy Jeakins, then only 24 years old, was Dryden's last assistant. In 1938 it was her first job in the film industry and she has recorded her memory of this time with affection.

The studio where we worked was called General Service (part of Paramount Pictures via Emmanuel Cohen productions). It was one of the oldest built in Hollywood. It was pleasant. I rode the bus or walked three miles each way to get there . . . I had a dog Dryden adored: an Irish setter named Dan. He was killed by an automobile. Dryden was so upset that he insisted the dog be cremated ($50) at his expense and taken to a pet cemetery. The dog was all I had.

Through her young eyes, which had not yet seen Europe, we see Dryden as he then was, as someone to work with, and the difficulties he had with deadlines, and with uncompromising or temperamental stars, such as Mae West in particular. She continues: 'He had made period clothes for Mae West after she threw out what Schiaparelli had made for her . . . she was difficult, impossible to please and she drove him MAD.' Amusingly, Dorothy Jeakins also records that Dryden was 'not easy to please either'.

Dorothy Jeakins, whose own career reads like a roll call of the greatest films since 1940, has spoken of her debt to Dryden and of the encouragement he gave her which led to her first break. 'He introduced me to a world of elegance, of style, of sophistication, of handsome glamorous women and what it was that made them so . . . I remember and am for ever grateful for his patience . . .'

FROM RURITANIA TO SHANGRI-LA

If the Austria that Dryden came from could be regarded as Ruritania, then certainly Hollywood must have seemed to him like Shangri-la. Interestingly, out of the nine films Dryden worked on, two of them are set in these mystical countries. On these and other films the variety of settings was enormous. What could be more different than the costumes which had to be created for *Lost Horizon* (1937), *The Prisoner of Zenda* (1937), and *The Garden of Allah* (1936), and the totally homespun requirements of *The Adventures of Tom Sawyer* (1937)?

His charming designs for Tom and Huck show how Dryden was able to absorb the lively American-ness of this most American of tales. A useful insight into how Dryden may have worked is provided by the typed character notes, which still survive, presumably supplied by the studio. For Tom and Huck they read:

TOM Beguiling, mischievous, essentially good, but very imaginative boy. Curly blond hair that won't stay plastered down.
HUCK FINN Skinny, ragged and dirty . . . undernourished . . . keen eyes . . . no definite coloring. . . but freckled . . . generally thought red-haired.

Dryden also created Becky, the school Teacher, Injun Joe and all the other minor parts and even, in this case, the traditional hair-do's.

Frank Capra's *Lost Horizon* (1937), on the other hand, the film on which Harry Cohen gambled four times the budget of any previous Columbia film, presented a wholly different challenge: how to create in costume the nature of a society – Shangri-la – that has evolved in the Tibetan mountains in virtual isolation and peace for thousands of years. The art director of the film, Stephen Gooson, led the way with regard to architecture and scene design. But to Dryden fell the role of expressing the concept through the garments, the most frequently seen and yet ideally the least obtrusive part of any film. The answer seems to have been to create a costume that was neither eastern nor western; that is, one which could take some concepts from one and some from the other and re-evolve. For instance, the most obvious alteration was to dispense with collars. Collars were to be seen as a western anomaly, a formality unnecessary in a Utopian society at peace with itself. Also the garments for male and female would be closer to each other in materials and style. They would be of silk, mandarin style, almost pyjamas, suitable to be worn in the wide cool halls of the High Lama's palace. The High Lama himself was to be set apart, as befitted his status. He wore an eastern type mitre to symbolize his semi-religious, semi-secular position at the head of this society. The guards would wear animals skins and marvellous furs, with boots and hats of the same material for the trek across the mountains.

Finally the distinction would be made, as Ronald Colman escapes back to civilization, between society as we know it and Shangri-la. When he returns to civilization he is seen at a gentlemen's club, wearing black tie and surrounded by moustachioed members dressed with equal formality who listen to his weird account of that far-off world. Nothing could make the point of entering a new civilization more clearly than a change of costume, and the changing out of travelling clothes and into the national costume of Shangri-la is the opening scene as the tired and bewildered passengers of the Dakota aircraft enter the new land and are – in the nicest possible way – taken captive.

Sadly, many of the original designs are lost and the original costumes, as in almost all cases, have been destroyed. But in a warehouse at the premises of Western Costume Co in Los Angeles there remains one faint reminder of how these designs once looked in real life. There, thanks to the conservation instincts of an employee of that firm, lies a cupboard full of some of the most famous costumes ever to have been made. Erich von Stroheim's suit from *Sunset Boulevard* is one. Somewhere amongst that diminished rack of what now remains of Hollywood's costume history, its impromptu curator, who had collected together the garments for no other reason than reverence for the films, pulled out to show me the brown, quilted jacket Ronald Colman wore in *Lost Horizon*. This, probably the only extant example of a genuine Dryden costume, was saved from the fate of many others because of its strange design and because of its star. On the neck was Ronald Colman's name – misspelt as Ronald 'Coleman'.

So unusual were the costumes for this film that it spawned a separate industry

The label on the collar of the quilted jacket designed by Ernst Dryden for Ronald Colman in the film *Lost Horizon* (1937).

entirely – adaptations were made for retail sale at stores such as Saks, Macy's or Marshall Field. The designs were photographed by the press agencies as part of the general publicity for the film itself, giving rise to purple passages of descriptive prose such as the following description of a design adapted from a costume for Jane Wyatt – the character of Sondra – by one whom they describe as 'famed Parisian designer, Ernst Dryden'. 'This frock of white wool has trim of leopard and neck piping of black wool. This is suggested as a smart cocktail frock for Fall.'

Lost Horizon was an immensely successful film that has lost none of its freshness even today. We are still mystified by other worlds, and in a recent conversation, the actress Jane Wyatt seemed as idealistic about it as the character she once portrayed. Perhaps Shangri-la really did exist – somewhere in the ice-house and lots that were used to create it?

But Hollywood also had something else on its mind in the years 1935-36. The rumoured love affair between Edward VIII and an American divorcee followed by the abdication a year later. Indeed, it was an event to cause David Selznick to take up studying history. Never far from its perennial obsession with royalty (as a setting or backdrop for worldly melodrama) in the Edward and Mrs Simpson story Hollywood had a real life evolving screenplay. Hearing that the author of *The Garden of Allah*, Robert Hichens had a villa of the same name, this was immediately loaned to the honeymoon couple while producers went scurrying for their history books to find stories that could be adapted to the screen to reflect this real life drama.

Two royalty films of this moment, both of which Dryden worked on, were Josef von Sternberg's *The King Steps Out* (1937) and *The Prisoner of Zenda* (1937), which shared the themes of the common person's unexpected elevation to Royal status. In *The Prisoner of Zenda* they found a story which had been popular on the screen as early as 1922, the story of the lookalike tourist with ordinary homespun values (played by Ronald Colman) who comes to the rescue of the debauched reputation of the throne by doubling as the King at his coronation until the real King returns to his senses.

The King Steps Out was a story closer to home for Dryden, for it was the true story of the Austrian princess Cissy who came from a relatively poor family in Bavaria only to ascend to the throne as consort to the Emperor and become Empress of Austria. The requirement from Dryden in both cases was for a large quantity of period costumes. On *The King Steps Out* his role may have been more extensive as, apart from the numerous costume designs, a small number of scene designs survive too. So accurate are they, that they tally exactly with specific scenes in the film, suggesting that on this film, owing to his special knowledge of Austrian uniform and personal knowledge of Hapsburg Austria, he was working closely with its director. Once again in this light operatic comedy, which was a vehicle for the talents of the singer-actress Grace Moore, costume was an intrinsic part of the plot. The silver dress Cissy carries in a box as she arrives from the country dressed in her rural clothes is to transform her from country maiden to Empress of all Austria-Hungary.

In *The Prisoner of Zenda* the requirement, as in *Lost Horizon*, was for a world that did not quite exist, except in popular imagination – Ruritania. Dryden based most of the costumes on Hapsburg Austria, perhaps perceiving that as far as Hollywood was concerned the distinction between a central European country which did exist and one that did not was marginal. The main aim as ever was the creation of a world which would be believed. With Dryden's extensive

Two sketches in pencil and watercolour from *The King Steps Out* (1937) showing scenes as they appeared in the film.

knowledge of European costume and custom this was not difficult to create. The ladies, on the other hand, owed their costume more to Hollywood than to any central European monarchy. Madeleine Carroll's off-the-shoulder gown as Flavia was certainly in the style of Mrs Simpson had she been Queen of England. For a nation of Republicans the costume captured the spirit of the moment which Americans had yearned would happen – that one of their number would indeed be elevated to become Queen.

Although the script does not mention England at all, except as the place that Ronald Colman comes from, most of the cast, which also included David Niven, Douglas Fairbanks Jr, Raymond Massey and Sir Charles Aubrey Smith, were British. It was the Royal Wedding everyone had been denied, and Dryden had been commissioned as dressmaker to the imaginary Queen.

Dryden's career in Hollywood could have gone on much longer. Although his letters reveal his tiredness and growing anxiety about Europe, his friends of the time never saw or remarked on a trace of it. One of them, a young Billy Wilder, was yet to write his first movie, but was working on his first script for Ernst Lubitsch – the film that became *Bluebeard's Eighth Wife*.

On the evening of 16 March 1938 Dryden had agreed to meet a small party of friends – Bronislaw Kaper, the Polish composer, and his wife Lola and Billy Wilder – for the preview of *Bluebeard*. Dryden did not turn up, and when the party left the preview and dinner at 10.00 pm they heard on the radio that Dryden had been found dead in his home, of a heart attack.

Billy Wilder has commented recently as follows: 'He was making it and I had not yet. Why should he have liked me? I was nothing at this stage. But he surrounded himself not with stars, but people he felt something for. In a certain sense I am in his debt for his advice, for our many discussions. He had a lot of wisdom to share.'

From his letters it had appeared that Dryden was getting increasingly tired. He had always driven himself hard, and the unceasing competition and moves from country to country may well have drained his strength. Billy Wilder, however, regarded this time for Dryden differently: 'In a sense his Hollywood was the flowering of everything he did. It was not a decline, it was the peak. He was like someone who just started to waltz and having got half-way round the room dropped dead.'

We know one other detail about Dryden's death – that he had the radio next to his ear. He had known, better than any, what the cost of coming to the United States would be. He knew also of the danger that faced those who had stayed in Europe, which included both his brother and sister, neither of whom survived the war. It is possible to imagine the broken reports that must have been received in far-off Hollywood of events in Europe and, safe as he personally was, how those words must have stung.

So the career that began in the Austria of the Emperor ended within five days of Hitler's invasion of Vienna. In that period Dryden had scaled the peaks of no fewer than five separate media – posters, dress and menswear design, advertising, magazine covers and illustration, and Hollywood film costume design. Dryden's death came at the close of an era for Hollywood. There would be no more voluntary exiles before the war, and following 1945 a new and rather different film industry was to emerge, in which the role of the costume designer was much reduced and the role of the commercial artist as a whole was temporarily eclipsed.

**Portrait of a jazz player for the film
Dr Rhythm (1938) in pencil
and wash on paper.**

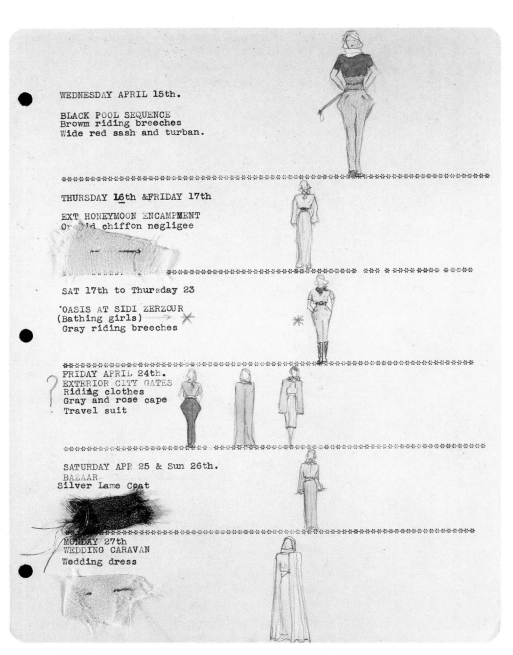

WEDNESDAY APRIL 15th.

BLACK POOL SEQUENCE
Brown riding breeches
Wide red sash and turban.

THURSDAY 16th &FRIDAY 17th

EXT HONEYMOON ENCAMPMENT
Orchid chiffon negligee

SAT 17th to Thursday 23

OASIS AT SIDI ZERZOUR
(Bathing girls)
Gray riding breeches

FRIDAY APRIL 24th.
EXTERIOR CITY GATES
Riding clothes
Gray and rose cape
Travel suit

SATURDAY APR 25 & Sun 26th.
BAZAAR
Silver Lame Coat

MONDAY 27th
WEDDING CARAVAN
Wedding dress

Page from Dryden's storyboard of *The Garden of Allah* (1936) showing a six-day shoot between April 15th and 27th, 1935 with silver lamé and chiffon samples attached. Dryden's miniature designs are in pencil and watercolour on paper.

Opposite
Marlene Dietrich and Charles Boyer on the set of *The Garden of Allah*. On the right director Richard Boleslavski is smoking a pipe and Ernst Dryden is seated with his back to the palm tree.

Costume design in pencil and watercolour on paper of a pink gown for Marlene Dietrich in *The Garden of Allah* (1936).

Opposite
Costume design in pencil and watercolour on paper for Marlene Dietrich's black satin dress in *The Garden of Allah* (1936).

Costume design in pencil and
watercolour on paper for a hostess in
The Garden of Allah (1936).

Costume design in pencil and
watercolour on paper of a red ball-
gown for the character of Flavia
played by Madeleine Carroll in *The
Prisoner of Zenda* (1937).

Previous pages
**Two costume designs in pencil and
watercolour on paper for Tilly Losch in
her role as dancer in *The Garden of
Allah* (1936).**

Costume design in pencil and watercolour on paper for Dolores del Rio in *The Devil's Playground* (1937).

Photographic still of a scene from the High Lama's palace in the film *Lost Horizon* (1937) showing Ronald Colman wearing the quilted jacket below and other costumes designed by Dryden.

Costume design in pencil and watercolour on paper for the character of Sondra (played by Jane Wyatt) in the film *Lost Horizon* (1937).

A costume design for the character of Huck Finn and another for 'Tom' from David Selznick's *The Adventures of Tom Sawyer* (1937).

*T*HE CHANCE survival of Ernst Dryden's work highlights the plight of the commercial artist in general. Because the commissions he executed were for a range of buyers whose specific purposes were of the moment and of their period, they were not expected to last. This is quite unlike the experience of fine artists, who are usually more closely concerned with posterity and are conscious of history and tradition in all that they do.

By contrast, while the commercial artist may draw ideas from the past, he is more interested in a different series of criteria — will a design work? will an advertisement be popular and sell more goods or enhance the image of the advertiser? will a costume design add to the glamour of a film? Perhaps the commercial artist was lucky that a set of tests existed against which his work had to be measured on a daily basis. He was utterly unlike the fine artist, who knew from the start that he might not see true appreciation of his art within his lifetime.

However, tastes and perspectives change. Dryden's career belongs to a vanished era which almost approximates to his own dates. It was a period in which a combination of social, artistic and economic circumstances combined to produce not only a demand for and production of commercial art, but also a massive audience for it. The gallery was not a closed room any more, but a street corner or a poster pillar on whose walls the latest images could be seen, or a newspaper or magazine with glorious illustration. Commercial art was an intrinsic part of daily life. The commercial artist in turn had a relationship to his mass audience which was close and powerful and wholly unlike today. And yet the reputation of the commercial artist was still handicapped, because his work was done for many different companies and usually existed only in published form, usually scattered among the ephemeral media for which he worked. As a poignant example of his era, the survival of Dryden's original designs and artwork, therefore, is a most rare event as it allows us to prove the point that commercial artists, while appearing fickle to the world at large, could and did remain consistent to themselves, exploring and producing under conditions of extreme pressure, designs which may now be seen as some of the most evocative images of the era. In Dryden's case one thinks of his advertisements for Cinzano and Bugatti or some of his cover illustrations for *Die Dame*.

Dryden belongs to a point in art history whose story is still being written and in which, so far, the commercial artist's position has not been fully valued. However, as the years pass and future generations return to this period to ask questions as to what it was like — what were the mass feelings which drove people, what entertained and interested them, and so on — it may finally be to the work of commercial artists like Dryden that they will turn.

To appreciate the commercial illustrator's once pivotal role in the world, one only has to pick up any magazine today, and remind oneself that in almost every case where there is now a photograph there would once have been a drawing. This is not to underestimate the achievements of photographers, but simply to note how Dryden's era ended. Another important change was that in the post-war era elegance was no longer regarded as an essential element of chic. In Dryden's time it would not have been possible to be chic without being elegant, and if the genius with which he was able to gild his designs may be said to be God-given, then may we say that his world was indeed *divinely elegant*.

Bernhard Denscher, *Tagebuch der Strasse*
(Österreicher Bundesverlag 1981)

Marlene Dietrich, *Ich bin, Gott sei Dank, Berlinerin*
(Ullstein 1987)

Dr Heinrich Fuchs, *Die Österreichischen Maler der Geburtsjahrgänge 1881–1900*
(Dr Heinrich Fuchs, Selbstverlag)

Max Gallo, *The Poster in History*
(American Heritage Publishing 1974)

Patricia Frantz Kery, *Art Deco Graphics*
(Thames & Hudson 1986)

Dan Klein, Nancy McClelland, Malcolm Haslam, *In the Deco Style*
(Thames & Hudson 1987)

Horst-Herbert Kossatz & Walter Koschatsky, *Ornamental Posters of the Vienna Secession*
(Academy Editions 1974)

Elizabeth Leese, *Costume Design in the Movies*
(Frederick Ungar 1976)

Arie Van de Lemme, *A Guide to Art Deco Style*
(Apple Press 1986)

Dr Ruth Malhotra, *Das frühe Plakat in Europa und den USA – Band 3*
(Gebr Mann Verlag 1980)

Theodore Menten, *Advertising Art in the Art Deco Style*
(Dover Publications 1975)

William Packer, *Fashion Drawing in Vogue*
(Thames & Hudson 1983)

Jack Rennert, *100 Poster Masterpieces*
(Phillips Auction House Catalogue 1981)

Walter Terry & Jack Rennert, *100 Years of Dance Posters*
(Avon Books 1975)

Sue Thompson, *Decorative Dressmaking*
(Rodale Press, Pennsylvania 1985)

Alain Weill, *The Poster – A Worldwide Survey and History*
(Sotheby's Publications 1985)

Hermann Wündrich, *Das Plakat als Werbemittel und Kunstprodukt*
(Monumental und Plakatreklame GmbH 1979)

Die Dame, eine Deutsches Journal für den verwöhnten Geschmack 1912-1943
(Verlag Ullstein 1980)

Contemporary book references and articles on Ernst Deutsch

Collection: Wiener Stadt und Landesbibliothek
Ottokar Mascha, *Österreichische Plakatkunst*
(Vienna 1915)

Collection: Institut für Zeitungsforschung der Stadt Dortmund
Hans Reimann, *Die Schwarze Liste*
(1916)

Collection: H. F. & P. H. Reemtsma GmbH, Hamburg
E.E. Hermann Schmidt, *Von Reklame und anderen Dingen* (About advertising & other matters)
(Das Kontor, Berlin 1918)

Collection: Kunstbibliothek, SMPK, Berlin
Mitteilungen des Vereins Deutscher Reklamefachleute
(Association of German Advertising Experts)
(Issue No 38, March 1913)

Includes articles:
Julius Klinger, 'Ernst Deutsch'
E. E. Hermann Schmidt, 'Deutsch und der Kauffmann'

Reference books: Ernst Deutsch

Thieme Becker, Künstler Lexikon, Volume 9
Benezit, Dictionnaire des Peintres, Sculptures, Dessinateurs et Graveurs
(Librairie Gründ 1976)

Das Frühe Plakat in Europa und den USA, Band 3, Deutschland,
1980,
Gebr, Mann Verlag, Berlin Kat Nr. 539

Albertina-Buch

Contemporary publications

1 With works accredited to Ernst Deutsch
Jugend 1911, 1912, 1913
Elegante Welt 1912
Deutsche Illustrierte Zeitung 1913
Seidels Reklame 1913
Lustige Blätter 1912

2 With works accredited to Ernst Dryden
Neue Freie Presse 1919
Gebrauchsgraphik 1929
Die Dame 1926-1933
French *Vogue* 1926-1929
Adam, La Revue de L'Homme 1930-1932

Mainly works pre-1919 signed *Deutsch*

Austria

Albertina Museum, Graphische Sammlung, Vienna
26 pieces. (20 signed Deutsch 1913 and undated,
6 signed Dryden 5 × 1919, 1 × 1920)

Österreichisches Museum für Angewandte Kunst, Vienna
34 pieces. 1911, 1912, 1916, 1920 & undated

Wiener Stadt und Landesbibliothek, Vienna
2 × 1923, 1 × 1919

Great Britain

Victoria & Albert Museum, London
11 pieces. 1912, 1919, 1928, 1934, 1936

Hiram Walker International Ltd, London
6 pieces c. 1928

Switzerland

Kunstgewerbemuseum der Stadt Zürich
5 pieces. 1912, 1913, 1914, 1916

West Germany

Staatsgalerie Stuttgart, Graphische Sammlung
41 pieces

Hessisches Landesmuseum Darmstadt
5 pieces. 1910, 1914 & 1915

Münchner Stadtmuseum
3 pieces. 2 × 1910, 1 × 1920

Stadtarchiv Landeshaupstadt München
1 piece. (Photographic record)

Kunstbibliothek SMPK, Berlin
51 pieces

Nürnberger Akademie für Absatzwirtschaft
Exact number not known. 1 × 1911, 1 × 1912

Deutsches Plakat Museum, Essen
5 pieces approx. Exact number not known

Deutsches Städte-Reklame GmbH, München
3 pieces. 1912, 1913, 1915

Kunstmuseum Hannover mit Sammlung Sprengel
1 piece 1913

Schiller Nationalmusuem, Marbach am Neckar
3 pieces (Book Covers). 1912, 1913, 1917

Museum für Kunst und Gewerbe, Hamburg
7 pieces

Private Collections

London, Strasbourg, New York, Hollywood

Book-Cover designs

Collection: Schiller Nationalmuseum

Felix Schloemp, *Der Perverse Maikaefer*
(1912)

Rideamus, *Lauter Lügen*
(1913)

Ernst Deutsch, *Galante Frauen*
(1917)

Archives

Kantonales Amt für Wirtschafts und Kulturausstellungen, Bern
Die Dame

Ullstein Archiv, Berlin
Complete record of *Die Dame*

Institut für Zeitungsforschung der Stadt Dortmund
Die Dame April-September   1930/1931
Die Dame October-April   1932/1933

Hans Reimann, *Die Schwarze Liste*
(Kurt Wolff Verlag, Leipzig 1916)

Condé Nast Publications Ltd, London
French *Vogue*

Picture credits

I would like to thank the following people without whom this book would not have been possible:

Lily Guttmann (née Krasa), Hello's sister and Dryden's friend; Ms Dorothy Jeakins, Dryden's last assistant; Mrs Madeleine Ginzburg and Ms Susan Lambert from The Victoria and Albert Museum; Dr John Whiteley of the Ashmolean Museum, Oxford; Miss Elizabeth Leese, author of *Costume Design in the Movies*; Mrs Sally Nelson-Harb and Mr Bert Granite of Western Costume Company, Los Angeles.

Further thanks are also due to the following, each of whom contributed in some way to my search for information on Ernst Dryden:

Mr Tim Black; Mr Harry Blacker; Mr Henry Brown; Ms Asya Chorley; Mr John Cobbett-Maddy; Mrs Zuleika Dobson; Dr Wolfgang Fischer; Mr Eric Kellenberger; Mr Klaus Martin Kersten; Mrs Elizabeth Kessler-Wellesz; Mr Miles Kington; Mr Peter Knize; Dr Ann Marie Koller; Mr Mickey Mishne; Mr William Packer; Mr Hector Paterson; Mr Hans Polak; Dr Klaus Popitz; Mr Hans Georg Puchert; Mr Jack Rennert; Ms Minerva Resendez; Mr Phillippe Rogivue; Mr Richard Schickel; Mr Bruce Smeaton; Mr Stephen Sondheim; Mr John Russell Taylor; Mr and Mrs Frederick Ullstein; Mr Alain Weill; Mr and Mrs Billy Wilder.

I would also like to acknowledge the help of the late Mr Victor Skutezky, the late Mrs Regina Reynold and the late Mrs Trude Rachlitz.

Thanks also to the following institutions:

The Bugatti Owners Club; Canadian Club Whisky; Cinzano; The Friends of Gabriel Voisin; The Graphische Sammlung Albertina, Wien; The Imperial War Museum, London; Knize & Company; The Kriegsarchiv Wien; The Kunstbibliothek, SMPK, Berlin; The Magistrat der Stadt Wien; The Österreichisches Museum für Angewandte Kunst, Wien; Reemstma Cigarettenfabriken GmbH; The Thirties Society; Ullstein Verlag, Berlin; W & F C Bonham & Sons Ltd.

I would also like to thank my secretary, Sue Adams.